Amazing Grace for the Catholic Heart

Amazing Grace
for the Catholic Heart

101 Stories of Faith,
Inspiration, Hope, and Humor

Edited by
Jeff Cavins, Matthew Pinto, and
Patti Maguire Armstrong

ASCENSION
P R E S S

West Chester, Pennsylvania

Ascension Press, LLC
Post Office Box 1990
West Chester, PA 19380
Orders: (800) 376-0520
www.AscensionPress.com

Cover design: Kinsey Caruth

Printed in the United States of America

ISBN 0-9659228-7-1

To my daughter Carly. You have captured my heart. I will love you forever

— Jeff Cavins

To all priests and teachers of the Catholic Faith. May you continue to be a source of grace and truth to the world. Thank you for your commitment to Christ and the Church.

— Matthew Pinto

To my husband, Mark, and my children—my eight blessings: Aaron, Luke, Tyler, Jacob, Mary, Teresa, John, and Isaac, and also to my bonus blessing, our foster boy from Kenya, Calvin Motika.

— Patti Maguire Armstrong

Contents

Chapter 2 — Family Matters

Chapter 3 — He Picked Me Up When I Was Down

Chapter 4 — The Lighter Side of Grace

Chapter 5 — His Healing Touch

Chapter 6 — Life is Precious

Chapter 7 — Expect the Unexpected

Introduction

Grace cannot be seen, touched, or otherwise perceived by our senses. Yet, we Catholics believe it is as real as the words on this page. Grace gives supernatural life to our souls, empowers us to live virtuous lives, and transforms our hearts. Grace is truly amazing.

The proof of grace is found not only in Scripture and the *Catechism*, but in the lives of everyone who has ever lived, including your own life! The dozens of people whose stories appear in this book have experienced miraculous events, divine interventions, and sublime joys that could only have come from the source of all grace, God Himself.

Our God is a God of truth, miracles, love, and laughter. And our faith in Him should not be stoic and sterile, but a reality to be embraced with joy and perseverance. This, ultimately, is the message in each story in this book. Our God can turn tears into laughter, lift us up when we are down, turn around even the bleakest situation, and bring extraordinary joy to our lives.

Amazing Grace for the Catholic Heart is a collection of stories of faith, inspiration, hope and humor. It is a "retreat in a book"—a place for you to turn when you need a "faith lift." By preparing and collecting these stories, our hope is to help you celebrate your Catholic faith—and experience God's amazing grace—like never before.

Consider this book to be a family album of sorts. The stories within are those of your brothers and sisters in faith. Many of the grace-filled experiences contained within may bear a striking resemblance to your own experiences. After all, we are one body in Christ, connected to one another through our common baptism. So sit back, kick up your feet, and enjoy this celebration of grace, faith, and family.

— Jeff Cavins, Matthew Pinto, and Patti Maguire Armstrong

Chapter 1
With God All Things Are Possible

The Badge of Grace

In the spring of 1967, my younger brother was reported missing in action in Vietnam. Although it was just a clerical error on the part of the Marines, it gave us all a horrible fright. First, we received a telegram stating Mike was missing in action. Then another informing us Mike had lost his legs and was in critical condition. Then followed the nightmare of a Marine officer and chaplain arriving on my parents' doorstep with the news Mike had died.

It turned out Mike was actually recuperating from a minor wound in Tokyo, Japan. He called soon after we received the mistaken report.

It was at this point that my older brother Bill determined to put college on hold and rejoin the Marines. He asked for duty in Vietnam to be with my younger brother Mike. His hope was to convince Mike to file under the Sullivan ruling, which states no more than one family member has to serve in a life-threatening situation at a time.

Bill wanted Mike in a safer place—out of the combat zone—while he served in 'Nam himself. Bill had always looked out for his three younger siblings, and he was determined to do so again. If Mike refused to leave, Bill figured they could at least support one another.

The last thing my father did on the day Bill was to leave for retraining was to make sure he was wearing his

Sacred Heart badge. My parents had my sister, two brothers, and me consecrated to the Sacred Heart when were babies. They made sure we made the First Friday devotions that were given to St. Margaret Mary. It was to her that Christ revealed his promises concerning devotion to His Most Sacred Heart.

Daddy jokingly told Bill: "It might not stop a bullet, but it can keep you safe along the way. Just remember it is only as good as the faith you put with it. If you wear it as a scrap of material and don't follow Christ, it will be no help at all. Remember what's important ... Trust Christ and follow him. He will get you home. Ask St. Margaret to help you too. That's all the protection you really need." With that last bit of unassuming faith from my father, Bill left for boot camp wearing the banner of Christ, his Sacred Heart badge.

After training, Bill landed in Vietnam on August 21st. Sadly, the very day Bill landed, our brother Mike was again wounded. This time his wounds were much more serious. A land mine struck his amphibious mobile unit and Mike was badly burned. Bill managed to track him down in a hospital in Dong Hoa.

Because of the severity of Mike's wounds, Bill was not allowed in to see him. All Bill could do was say a prayer and report for duty. The two never saw each other before Mike was soon transported stateside for medical treatment. Bill's plans were to do his duty, and then return home to finish college. He had a sense of duty to serve his country, and he strove to follow Christ even under difficult circumstances.

In order not to worry us, Bill wrote letters home telling us he was assigned in Da Nang as a clerk. He jokingly referred to his great quest to serve as being reduced

to shuffling papers. That was our Bill—always protecting others. His ploy worked, and we believed that he
was fairly safe in Da Nang.

But then, during the night of September 21, 1967, I
had a terrible dream. I dreamed I was standing on a small
incline and saw my brother Billy carrying a machine gun.
I heard the horrible sound of rockets and mortars going
off. In my dream I screamed: "Run, Billy, run!" And then
a big flash and explosion landed close to him. Through
the smoke and fire I saw him lying wounded. Both of his
hands were gone and there was blood everywhere. He
was moaning in pain but I could not reach him. My heart
broke as I watched and tried to run to him. My beloved
Billy was all alone. I was so close to him and yet so far.

Then, suddenly, I saw a Catholic chaplain run over to
Bill. He appeared to be wounded also but leaned over Bill
and began to comfort him. He prayed and anointed Bill as
best he could. He was so calm and reassuring to my brother. He said: "Don't worry son. God is with us this good
day." I was crying so hard by this time, I woke up from
this awful nightmare. As I always did as a child, I wanted
my dad to sooth me from this nightmare. I got out of bed
and called him at 1:30 a.m.

When I called, the phone barely rang once before
Dad picked it up. He was crying softly when he
answered. To this day I don't remember which one of us
said it first: "Billy is dead." Dad and I related the exact
same dream and the exact details. We consoled one another, and clung to the hope that it was just a warning.
"Maybe it is just a sign we need to pray harder for Bill,"
Dad said. We both so desperately wanted to believe that.

One week later, on September 28th, the Marines
again paid a visit to my parent's home. This time there

would be no phone call saying it was a mistake. Instead, our nightmare was confirmed. Billy was dead.

The Marines reported that on September 21ˢᵗ, while on night patrol, Bill's entire unit was caught in an ambush. They were trapped in a crossfire of rocket and mortar fire, which claimed the life of every man in the unit. Bill managed to survive alone until another unit found him. One of the letters we received later related how the Marines, who ministered first aid to Bill before he died, had promised to honor Bill's request: "Please thank the Padre for helping me die well." They unfortunately did not know the name of the priest who had administered the last rites of the Church to Bill. There wasn't one in their unit.

We were told Bill was at peace when he died on September 21ˢᵗ, exactly one month from the day that he had landed in Vietnam. Christ kept his promise to protect those devoted to His Most Sacred Heart even deep in the jungles of Vietnam. We never could locate the chaplain who helped my brother. As time passed, we decided we would never be able to thank the mysterious priest in this life.

~

My beloved father went home to meet his Lord on Valentine's Day, 1985. Before he died, he gave me his most treasured possession—the tattered and bloodstained Sacred Heart badge which the Marines had returned after Bill's death. He asked that should I ever find that wonderful priest who had helped Bill, to thank him personally.

Many years had passed when I received an e-mail one day from a friend who had also served in Vietnam. He wanted me to read about a wonderful chaplain from Vietnam who received the Congressional Medal of Honor for his extraordinary service. The chaplain was known as the "Grunt Padre." As I opened the attachment and saw the picture of the priest, my heart skipped a beat. It was the priest from my dream of Bill's death, all those years before. My father and I had both described him to each other in the same exact detail. His name was Father Vincent Robert Capodanno. He also had died in Vietnam in 1967.

Reading the attachment, I learned that Father Capodanno had died of severe wounds. He was missing part of his right hand. The story explained the extent of his injuries. They were the same wounds of the priest in my dream.

The article stated that Father Capodanno was well-known for his council to his beloved troops. He was known to say: "God is with us this good day." It was unbelievable; those were the words he had said in my dream. Then reading the date of his death, I held in my breath, blinked, and looked at the date again. A shiver shot through me from head to toe: Fr. Capodanno had died seventeen days *before* Bill.

〜

As part of the communion of saints, Father Capodanno was truly "a priest forever in the order of Melchezidek." Father Capodanno was the man whom Christ sent to fulfill the promise of the Sacred Heart Devotion revealed to St. Margaret Mary: *I promise thee in the excessive mercy of My Heart that My all-powerful love will grant to those who communicate on the first Friday in nine consecutive months the grace of final penitence; they shall not die in My disgrace nor without receiving their sacraments; My Divine Heart shall be their safe refuge in this last moment.*

— Christine Trollinger

Christine Trollinger writes for pleasure from her home in Gladstone, Missouri. After working as an insurance agent for twenty years, she now enjoys maintaining the Adoration Society she founded at her parish, as well as building-up the parish library she helped establish. Christine is the mother of three grown children, a wife of thirty-nine years, the former host of the website Catholic Chronicles, *and the author of several grace-filled stories included in this book.*

See pictures for this story at www.AmazingGraceOnLine.net/Heart

Tabitha

Driving down the street headed for the Dairy Queen one afternoon, I could not get Tabitha out of my mind. The tragedy of this young girl's life played on my mind much like a repetitive song that relentlessly repeats a chorus and refuses to leave the brain.

Everyone in Dayton, Ohio, where I was working as a pastor at the time, was talking about Tabitha. Although a mere thirteen years old, she had been arrested for the murder of another teenage girl. But she was no cold-blooded murderer. Tabitha wanted nothing more than to put an end to the other girl's bullying—she would repeatedly hit Tabitha on the head with a brick. When the harassment only got worse, Tabitha went to her older brother for help.

"The next time she tries it," big brother advised, "run into the house and get a steak knife. Then, pretend you are going to stab her but just tap her on the shoulder with it. That will scare her and she'll leave you alone."

When the bullying occurred once again, Tabitha followed her brother's advice. But as she aimed the knife just above the other girl's shoulder, it accidentally pierced the jugular vein. With blood spurting out, the injured girl ran screaming down the street. Before she reached the end of the second block, she fell down dead.

The police were called and immediately arrested Tabitha, who was in shock and offered no resistance. It was a story that the local news sensationalized for days. The immense tragedy of this accident and its horrifying result played on the minds of the entire community.

"What a shame," everybody said. "How sad."

I was in the business of offering comfort and guidance, but here I was feeling just as inadequate as the next person. The sadness was overwhelming and my helplessness stung bitterly.

As I drove along, Tabitha consumed my thoughts. Unable to shake them off, I pulled my car to the side of the road and sat contemplating the enormity of it all. I wondered, if Jesus was in my place, what could He possibly do to help in this situation. "Lord, what would You do if You were here?" I prayed.

Deep from within my heart I heard these words: "If I were there, I would go down to her prison, wrap my arms around her and say, 'I love you, I love you.'" The answer was so clear. I thought, "As a Christian, I am the body of Christ; I am His arms, His legs, His hands ... His voice."

"Lord, if that is what you want me to do, I will do it," I prayed. I turned the car around and headed back into downtown Dayton. Once I found the jail, I walked up to the front desk.

"My name is Jeff Cavins and I want to see Tabitha," I announced to a surprised guard.

"No one is allowed to see her," the guard responded, and then paused and gave me a funny look.

"Did you say you are Jeff Cavins?"

"Yes," I answered.

"Did you lead an Emmaus Cursillo retreat for women a couple of weeks ago?"

"Yes, I did."

A big smile crossed his face. "My wife went on that retreat and her life has been changed." He thought a moment and then handed me a pen. "Here, sign this and I'll take you to see her."

"Wow!" I thought. "What an amazing coincidence. God is surely leading the way."

We walked down a stark corridor to an empty cell. There I was instructed to wait while he went to get Tabitha. At that moment, the enormity of my actions hit me. Only fifteen minutes earlier I was on my way to get an ice cream cone. Now, here I was, nervously sitting in a jail cell. After a few moments, the door creaked open and in walked a petite little girl, trembling with fear. I later learned she thought I was there to take her to prison.

As I looked into her scared eyes, I stepped toward her. "Tabitha, my name is Jeff and I was driving down the road thinking about you today. I asked the Lord what He would want me to do about you." Then, I walked over to her and put my arms around her. "Tabitha," I whispered. "From Jesus: I love you so much." She cried and I held her. I sensed that I had truly touched her by reaching out and loving someone who the world had discarded.

Tabitha stepped back and opened her hand to reveal a small, crumpled piece of paper. She unraveled it and showed me a Christian tract about accepting Jesus as your savior and asking Him into your life.

"I prayed this last night," Tabitha said. "And here you are today."

Jesus had come to put His arms around her and say, "Tabitha, I love you."

Realizing the Lord had used me to touch this young girl's life was very emotional. Although everyone in Dayton knew about Tabitha, no one had come to visit. It made me think: What good is it to be the body of Christ unless we are going to act like the body of Christ. If we would simply act like the body of Christ—be His arms,

His legs, His voice—lives would change. Christ is looking to us to do His work if we will simply yield to His will and take the risk of loving others. Once we do that, at any hour on any day, even on the way to the Dairy Queen, Jesus can use us.

— Jeff Cavins

Jeff Cavins is co-editor of the Amazing Grace *series. His biography appears at the end of the book.*

Going the Distance

"There is no way I'm going to make it," I thought. I was twenty-five miles into the South African Comrades, a fifty-four-mile ultra marathon, and my body was spent. The rhythmic pounding of one foot over the other continued automatically, but I was certain my glycogen levels were too low to keep it up much longer. It was 1994 and, after a ten-year hiatus from running, this was going to be my last big race.

In the early 1980s, I won three consecutive New York Marathons and the Boston Marathon in 1982. I qualified for the U.S. Olympic team in 1980 and 1984 and had set US track records in the 5K, 10K, and five-mile run. My 1981 marathon time of 2:08:13 was a milestone for U.S. runners at that time.

To say I was self-assured back then is an understatement. I would predict I was going to win a marathon or set a world record, and then I would go out and do it. I pushed myself relentlessly.

On more than one occasion, I actually collapsed at the finish and had to be revived. It was mind over matter and winning was what mattered. But sometimes, not even dogged determination could override physical reality. In 1978, while still in college and competing against Bill Rodgers in hot, humid temperatures, I collapsed at the finish. Some people were concerned enough to have the sacrament of last rites administered to me in the medical tent.

My endocrine system became so stressed over time that I eventually became plagued with chronic health problems. I consulted doctors all over the world before finally realizing that my competitive running days were over. My belief had always been that I could accomplish anything I put my mind to—and I usually did—but now I had to accept defeat over something that was beyond my control.

It was around this time that I began to turn to God and religion in a serious way. My human frailty perhaps led me to more fully understand that it is God (and not me) who is ultimately in control. It was what my mother and father had always taught me.

My parents were devout Catholics. That is actually what brought us to the United States from Cuba. My father was working on the construction of a planned community. The only thing left to build was the chapel. Fidel Castro stepped in and told them there would no longer be a need for churches in the new society he was building. The year was 1959. My father wanted no part of a "new" anything that did not include God. We soon moved to the United States, and he and my mom raised their four kids as practicing Catholics.

Like so many young adults, I drifted away from Mass and the sacraments but finally returned with a vengeance. My Catholic faith was no longer just window dressing but became something that pervaded every part of my life. Even my regular workouts now included praying all fifteen mysteries of the Rosary.

Despite my physical setbacks, there were short periods of improvement, only to then run poorly again. The few races I did enter, my performances were mediocre at best. Then, in 1993, my running consistently and steadily improved. "One last race," I thought when I heard about the South African Marathon. I would be thirty-six.

The old adrenaline surge pulsed through my body at the starting line. "I can do this," I thought confidently. But now, halfway through, I determined it was impossible. "I can't do this," I thought. It was at that point, it hit me: I really was "my old self" when I started the race. Not once had I thought to pray or call upon God. "I can't do anything without You, God," I realized.

"Lord, I'm putting this race in your hands," I prayed. I then began praying the rosary. My legs somehow kept going. When I was still going an hour later, I thought: "Maybe this *is* God's plan for me today."

When I crossed the finish line, I had outrun 12,000 other entrants, winning the fifty-four-mile marathon in five hours, thirty-eight minutes and thirty-nine seconds— nearly a record.

Knowing how I felt physically, it was pretty amazing that I even finished that race, let alone won it. Once I acknowledged it was not in my power to keep going, I put myself in God's hands. In the end, this is the only success that matters.

— Alberto Salazar

Alberto Salazar coaches boys track at Central Catholic High School in Portland, Oregon. He tries to influence them positively by stressing the importance of spirituality and praying before races. He also works as a sports marketing consultant with Nike and coaches a group of Olympic-aspiring runners.

See pictures of this story at www.AmazingGraceOnline.net/Heart

Fishing for Faith

One beautiful, sunny Father's Day in 1992, my husband, Jim, and I decided to spend the afternoon fishing along the Missouri River with our four children. We were joined by long-time friends the Thurns and their four children.

The warmth of the sun and good company made for a relaxing afternoon of snacking, visiting, and off-shore fishing. Jonathan, the oldest Thurn boy, was especially happy to be trying out his new fishing pole. So it was with great alarm that he noticed it missing shortly after he had cast and placed it securely in a pole holder. The pole holder stood firmly planted deep into the sand, but the pole was nowhere in sight. With everyone accounted for, it was clear no one else had taken the pole.

It was a brand-new pole and this was Jonathan's first time using it. In the middle of our agitation, our oldest daughter, Maja Lisa, who was then nine, confidently announced, "Mom, you always tell us to pray when we lose something. Let's all ask Jesus to help us find it now."

She was so confident that God would help. At that point, I was torn. Yes, it was true I always had the kids pray when we lost something at home, but this was the Missouri River!

I did not want her to be disappointed and look foolish. I also thought I was defending God and did not want to put Him to the test. Regardless, there was no stopping Maja Lisa's sure faith. She led the group prayer asking God to please help Jonathan find his fishing pole.

Immediately after we all prayed, Jonathan's father, Mark, cast his line into the river. It caught on something.

Mark quickly reeled it in as everyone watched. His hook had caught on another fishing line. To everyone's surprise, he pulled in Jonathan's new pole which also had a very large carp on the end of the line.

"I'm sorry, Lord," I laughed and then humbly resolved: "I won't second-guess You again or try to protect You. I realize now You can take care of yourself."

— Jan Fritzhuspen

Jan and her family live a simple life in Bismarck, North Dakota. She is a secular Franciscan who has home educated her four children for more than twenty years. Jan was recently captured by a new activity—fly fishing for mountain "brookies" (brook trout) and anticipates the lessons God will no doubt teach the Fritzhuspen family through this new adventure.

See pictures related to this story at www.AmazingGraceOnLine.net/Heart

God Used Him

Truck driver Ron Lantz, sixty-two, believes an impromptu prayer meeting led to his spotting the two Washington, D.C. area sniper suspects who had allegedly killed ten people before Lantz saw them at an interstate rest area in Maryland. The arrests of suspects John Allen Muhammad and John Lee Malvo undoubtedly saved lives. Law enforcement officials claim the pair had been plotting their next attack. But that does not bring Lantz much comfort.

"I'd like to have had it ended before that," laments Lantz. Still, he insists that God orchestrated the men's capture.

Lantz, a trucker for more than thirty years, would listen to talk radio during his regular haul from Kentucky to Maryland. He was horrified at the news of each sniper attack. During one of these trips he decided to do something about it.

"I was on a CB radio talking to drivers," he said "and I asked them if they would follow me into this rest area and have a little prayer service about our country and about the snipers.

"Lo and behold, about fifty truckers were there. It took about fifty-eight minutes to have the prayer meeting. I just thought these people had to be caught some way or the other and that somebody was going to catch them."

The next Wednesday—October 23rd—Lantz was called in to work on his day off. Looking back, he can see God's hand in the events that followed.

That day, he was stopped by police three separate times but was not ticketed. With each stop he was delayed a few minutes while the cops checked his paperwork. "I've been driving a truck for thirty-six years and that's never happened before," he noted.

The same day, Lantz heard a description of the snipers' car. "I got down next to Baltimore on I-95. They described the car, the people in it, and the license-plate number. I wrote it down," said Lantz.

On his return trip to Kentucky he pulled into a rest area on Interstate 70 in Frederick County, Maryland, and immediately recognized the Chevrolet Caprice the police were looking for. Muhammad was asleep inside the car, and Malvo was resting on a park bench.

Lantz immediately placed an emergency call and waited for the police to arrive. An officer who responded told Lantz to use his rig to block the exit. Lantz then got on his CB radio and asked another trucker to block the entrance. He said he wasn't worried about his own safety.

"I wasn't scared," Lantz said. "I mean, the person I am, I'm not scared because the good Lord just put me there to do what I did."

Until 1997, Lantz had stayed away from church. That year, he promised his dying adult son that he would commit his life to serving God. Lantz did not realize it, but hours before he spotted the alleged snipers, a group at his church had held a prayer meeting of their own and had prayed for the killer's capture.

Fifteen minutes after Lantz made his 911 call, the area was swarming with police. They used a flash grenade to disorient the suspects before grabbing them both.

In his column for *The Wall Street Journal*, Brendan Miniter wrote: "Mr. Lantz offers us a simple but powerful story, one that reveals an underlying strength in American society that the media often neglect: Religious character matters. It's no coincidence that the best defenders of our domestic security are also turning out to be some of our most upstanding, moral citizens."

Although the FBI, state police, local law enforcement, and the best and latest technology were at work, God used a truck driver to bring this terror to an end.

Reprinted with permission from Charisma *magazine.*

The Lord's Little Helper

"I give up," I thought, turning off the computer. "I need to get some sleep." Several hours searching the Internet that evening had been in vain.

As president of my Blue Army chapter (an apostolate which promotes the Rosary) someone had contacted me regarding an organization that was bringing a pilgrim virgin statue into the diocese. I was certain the organization was not in union with its local bishop but I could not find anything to back this up.

I was already busy babysitting our nine-month-old granddaughter, but I still spent several hours searching for any reliable information that I could give to our spiritual director. It occurred to me that if there was anyone who would have such information, it would be Fr. Robert Fox, founder of the Fatima Family Apostolate. I had several years of Fr. Fox's *Immaculate Heart Messenger* magazines stored away in my basement but was too tired and too busy to take the time to search through them.

I said a prayer and decided to get some sleep. The next morning, I was still watching my granddaughter, Erin, who had recently started to crawl. She was not very familiar with our home and had spent most of her time on our living room floor. I happened to go into my office for something and Erin followed me. She went right over to the bottom shelf of a bookcase, pulled out a magazine, and came over to me at the desk and handed it to me.

To my surprise it was one of Fr. Fox's magazines. I opened it up and there was the article that I had been searching for the night before.

It took my breath away to realize that God had answered me through one so small and helpless as my baby granddaughter.

— Janet Helbing

Janet, a third order Carmelite who lives in Mandan, North Dakota, has three grown children and three grandchildren. She is president of the Blue Army for the Diocese of Bismarck. Her husband, Doug, is in the diaconate formation program.

The Little Girl in White

It was World War II when Eldon Dahl, a schoolmate of my husband's and a pilot in the United States Air-Force, was shot down over Italy. He was returning from a bombing raid near Foggia, Italy, on August 25, 1943. Parachuting from his flaming B-17 bomber, which was riddled with bullets from German fighter planes, he landed near a small Italian village. His parachute had landed him safely in a forest, but he was soon captured by the Italians. After being in two prison camps, Eldon managed to escape into the mountains north of Rome with a group of other Allied prisoners.

Eldon became separated from the others and wandered alone on foot through mountains and villages. Scavenging around the woods one afternoon, his empty stomach detected the wonderful aroma of food cooking on an open fire. Following the scent, he discovered two women outside, preparing food near a farm.

Hoping they would be friendly and willing to feed him, Eldon made his way toward the women. All of a sudden, a little blonde-haired girl around ten years old, wearing a bright white dress, appeared by his side. She motioned with a finger over her lips to remain quiet. Then, taking him by the hand, the little girl led him in the opposite direction to stand behind a thicket of bushes. It was at that point that two German soldiers appeared and began talking with the women. Eldon realized then that he had just narrowly avoided recapture. When he looked around the little girl had vanished. She was nowhere to be seen.

Eldon was convinced the little girl in white was his guardian angel. The knowledge that his guardian angel was with him gave him hope that he would somehow get back home.

For two months Eldon traveled alone for more than two hundred miles on foot before his final breakthrough of the turbulent front lines to return to the American zone near Cassino on November 13, 1943. Two weeks later he returned to the United States.

Eldon always credited the little girl in white, an angel of God, with saving him and guiding him safely home.

— Doris Fischer

Doris Fischer is the mother of four grown children, a housewife and a retired nurse. She has worked in hospitals and nursing homes for thirty years and served as a cadet nurse in the Army during WWII. She and her late husband, who passed away in 1999, were married for fifty-three years. Doris lives in rural North Dakota.

See pictures for this story at www.AmazingGraceOnLine.net/Heart

Vow of Silence?

"Finding it difficult to keep your
vow of silence, Brother Stanislaus?

Inspired by a Martyr

Ted Wojtkowski, seventy-five, considers himself a regular guy. He came to Chicago from Poland after World War II, worked as an engineer and raised a family in a nice home in the suburbs. But as a young man, he was privileged to witness one of the greatest acts of saintly heroism of the twentieth century. His encounter with spiritual greatness changed his life.

The year was 1939. In September, German tanks rumbled into Poland. The first village attacked by the Nazis was the home of Wojtkowski, then a 20-year-old student. A patriot, Wojtkowski went underground. He and his buddies manned a shortwave radio to gather war news from London and then secretly printed leaflets to let villagers know what was occurring.

Before long, Wojtkowski hopped on his father's bicycle and headed toward Hungary. His destination was France, where he hoped to joint the Polish army. The Nazis caught him at the border, jailed him, and sent him to Auschwitz on May 1, 1940.

Auschwitz was not a killing ground for Jews yet; the Nazis were using it then for criminals and for foes of their regime, including priests and activists. Wojtkowski, living with eight-hundred men in a two-story barracks, was put to work building more barracks. The Nazis treated the prisoners brutally. Priests were especially singled-out for punishment—guards kicked them in the face and stomach and clubbed them over the head. When a prisoner escaped, all the others were ordered to stand in the sun for days, hands on their heads. After a second escape, ten prisoners were machine-gunned. The third escape occurred on or about July 28, 1941.

One hundred members of Wojtkowski's barracks were forced to stand in rows of ten. Ten of them would die. Wojtkowski stood in the eighth row.

The camp commander ordered each row, one after the other, to step forward. He began a random selection. One, two, three were pulled from a group. Wojtkowski hoped that ten would be singled out before his row was reached.

A fourth, fifth, and sixth were picked. The sixth broke down. "My wife, my children ... " he sobbed. "Who will take care of them?" A prisoner from the sixth row turned to the commander. "I will take the place of this man with the wife and children," he said. Most remarkable of all was the volunteer's demeanor.

"His expression was so serene, so peaceful, not a shadow of fear," Wojtkowski recalls. The commander, however, was not impressed. "You must be some kind of (*expletive*) priest," he snarled. But he accepted him as one of the ten. The volunteer and nine others were locked in a bunker. The Nazis would not waste bullets on them: They would be starved to death.

The man was indeed a priest, but not just any priest. He was Franciscan Father Maximilian Kolbe. Poles considered Kolbe a saint. His personal assistant, Brother Jerome Wierzba, once said of him: "He had something good in his face that emanated God. Just looking at him gave you peace of mind."

Kolbe published religious magazines and newspapers read by more than one million Poles. He was widely admired, running the largest Catholic religious house in the world. Intensely devoted to the Blessed Mother, Kolbe supervised six-hundred-fifty friars at his City of the Immaculata, an evangelization center near Warsaw. The Nazis naturally regarded Kolbe with suspicion after they invaded Poland. When he resisted pressure to apply for German citizenship, for which he was eligible, he was arrested on February 17, 1941.

When the guards were out of ear shot, the prisoners shared information with one another about the fate of the ten in the bunker. Kolbe was leading the doomed in prayers and hymns, and a piece of bread had been smuggled in to be used in a Mass.

After three weeks, Kolbe was the last to die. The Nazis, impatient to use the bunker to punish others, had a doctor inject poison into Kolbe to finish him off.

The more Wojtkowski thought about Kolbe's self-sacrifice, the more astounded he was. Francis Gajowniczek, whom Kolbe had saved, was a peasant farmer. Kolbe, forty-seven, was one of the most accomplished men in Poland, a priest with many plans. Already he had begun a missionary center in Japan and was determined to open an evangelization center on each continent.

And Kolbe, who possessed great drive and ambition, had given up all his dreams in a moment. He truly was a man of God, Wojtkowski realized.

Kolbe saved not only Gajowniczek, but also Wojtkowski. Years of deprivation in Nazi camps awaited Wojtkowski. There would be backbreaking labor and physical abuse. But Wojtkowski never lost his will to survive.

"Father Kolbe inspired me," he says. "After his sacrifice, I never thought I would die at Auschwitz. Someday I would be liberated and tell what happened."

Wojtkowski finally gained his freedom in 1945. He was being marched to Dachau when he fled on foot. He took refuge with a German priest, who hid him and fed him until he regained his strength and the Allies rolled into Germany.

Today, Wojtkowski lives in Squeak, a Chicago suburb with a large Jewish population, including many Holocaust survivors. He prays often to Kolbe and keeps a huge scrapbook on him. In it are a piece of clothing worn by the priest before his arrest, an original signature from a daily Mass log, and an envelope once mailed by the priest. A painting of Kolbe hangs in Wojtkowski's study.

In the early 1970's, Wojtkowski recounted the events at Auschwitz to Vatican officials. His testimony was gathered as part of the canonization process. Kolbe was declared a saint in 1982 by his compatriot, Pope John Paul II, who declared him a martyr of charity.

In 1975, Wojtkowski, then president of the Polish Association of Former Political Prisoners, spearheaded the construction of a monument to Kolbe for the Carmelite Fathers in Munster, Indiana. An engineer, Wojtkowski designed the monument, which shows Kolbe pointing toward the nearby Marian grotto and holding his heart, in which are ashes from Auschwitz. A plaque on the statue reads, "We lived through it to tell the truth."

— Jay Copp

Jay Copp is a part-time freelance writer and a full-time communications manager for a non-profit organization. He lives near Chicago with is wife, Laura, and three young sons.

Chicken Runs at Midnight

As third base coach for the Pittsburgh Pirates in 1992, I was at the top of the world. Although it was only March, it was obvious we had a strong team and could expect a winning season.

But with one phone call, my world suddenly shattered. "Dad, I have something to tell you," my seventeen-year-old daughter, Amy, began. "Don't be mad at me."

With an opening like that, a hundred possibilities crossed my mind: she wrecked the car, drugs, pregnancy, bad grades ...

"What is it?" I asked, impatient for the bad news.

"Dad, I have a brain tumor."

I froze. No! I could not be hearing right. Not a brain tumor. Not my Ames.

"Dad, I'm sorry," she said breaking the silence.

"Sorry? What do you have to be sorry for?" I choked into the receiver. But that was Amy. She was thinking about her Dad rather than herself.

As the only girl among three brothers, Amy grew up to be one tough kid. When she was little, she loved to have me ask her: "Where do you want to go today?" Then, wherever she answered, I'd throw her giggling across the room onto the bed followed by the inevitable plea of, "Do it again, Daddy!"

But underneath her softly freckled face and strawberry blonde hair beat a heart of gold. Often I came home to find our garage full of neighborhood children playing school with Amy. She loved kids and dreamed of being a school teacher one day.

Amy was my number one fan. Baseball meant a lot to her because it meant a lot to me. Even though she could not come to the games, she decorated the house with orange and black pom poms, wore Pirate tee-shirts and watched the games on television. We missed each other so much.

When the Pirates won the National League championship that year, Amy flew out to attend the fifth game of the playoffs with the Atlanta Braves. It was not easy; her body was weakened from chemotherapy, her head bald, but she was still full of life as she cheered enthusiastically. Winning this game was the icing on the cake of having my number one fan there.

After the game, Amy leaned over while I was driving the car and asked, "Dad, when there's a man at second and you get down in your stance and cup your hands, what are you telling him? 'Chicken runs at midnight'?"

I laughed so hard I almost drove off the road. "Chicken runs at midnight? Where did you come up with that?" I asked. Amy laughed with me and said, "I don't know where it came from. It just came out." It was total nonsense, but it was totally Amy.

Amy had to return home to Arlington, Texas for treatment so she was unable to travel for the final game in the playoff series. But when I got to the stadium, someone handed me a phone message from her. It read: "Dear Dad, Chicken runs at midnight. Love, Amy."

As I was holding the note, the second baseman, Jose Lind, who spoke very little English, noticed me looking at it. "What's that?" he asked. "Chicken runs at midnight," I answered with a chuckle. He said, "Okay." Then as he went out onto the field, he ran around telling all the players, "Chicken runs at midnight. Chicken runs at midnight," not knowing what he was saying. Soon, in the dugout the whole team was saying, "Chicken runs at midnight. Let's go, chicken runs at midnight."

Amy was at home with her younger brother Tim, watching the game on television when they heard one of the players yell, "Chicken runs at midnight!" They screamed and howled with laughter.

From that point on, it became an ever-present family motto. We'd start and end phone conversations with it. When a newspaper photographer laughed about my funny stance in the team picture, I told him about the "Chicken runs at midnight" phrase that had come from it. He sent me an enlarged photograph with those five words boldly printed underneath.

Those five silly words took on a meaning all their own. They meant absolutely nothing, but to our family they came to mean everything. "Chicken runs at midnight" represented the love, the bond, the sense of humor and the baseball we all shared. They also represented Amy, and we were losing her fast.

We lost that final game and with it went my dream of going to the World Series. The loss hurt deeply. It was my last chance to share that dream with Amy. Three months later she lapsed into a coma.

I had been praying so hard for Amy to make it. I never wanted anything more in my life. Through her illness, I had regained the faith of my youth. Although many teens drift from religion, I was an oddity. Those were the years I went to daily Mass, prayed novenas and rosaries, and was even a pontifical server, which meant I served for the bishop.

In my twenties, religion took a backseat to baseball. By the time I was forty, I was no longer attending Mass just because it was inconvenient. But at forty-six, when Amy got her brain tumor, my world turned upside down and God ended up on top.

Sure, I pleaded and begged God to heal my little girl. But I also found the faith of my youth again. I knew that Amy would be in God's care regardless. When it came time to say good bye, I walked in the hospital room and held her. Tears poured down my face as I hugged Amy close and thanked her. Her dream of becoming a teacher would never come to pass but she had taught me so much. Through Amy I learned about love and joy and courage—right up until the very end. Although I could never really be ready to say good bye to my Ames, I was ready to accept God's will.

~

Amy died on January 28, 1993. The family all agreed on the words for her headstone: "Chicken runs at midnight." The lady at the funeral parlor initially tried to steer us in another direction. Something a little more dignified, I suppose. But it had to be "Chicken runs at midnight." To us, that phrase said it all. It kept us connected to the best of Amy.

As we planned for the funeral, I was distraught to learn Fr. David Yetsko, newly transferred to the St. Maria Goretti Church in Arlington, would be saying the Mass. He had never known Amy. He had no idea how special she was. When we met for the first time to plan the Mass, I was surprised to learn Fr. David was from Pittsburgh. I quickly discovered he was a big Pirates fan, but rarely had the chance to go to any games. He did manage to make it to one game the previous season, however. It was the same one that Amy was at, the one where the "Chicken runs at midnight" motto was born.

When we realized the incredible coincidence, Fr. David held my hands and we wept together. It turned out that he was just the right priest to say the Mass. His eulogy truly captured Amy's beauty. He even managed to include "Chicken runs at midnight" in it.

Four years later, in 1997, I went south to coach the Florida Marlins. We upset the Atlanta Braves in six games to win the National League championship. The dream I held since I was a little boy then became a reality. We were going to the World Series against the Cleveland Indians.

Although the Indians were favored to win, we held our own. After six games, the series was tied. My son Tim, who had just graduated from high school, was a bat boy at all six of the games. Then, for the last big game, another son, Mike, was able to take time away from college football to also put on a bat boy uniform.

The word "tense" does not describe this final face-off. In the ninth inning, the Marlins tied the score, sending the game into extra innings. In the bottom of the eleventh, with two outs, we needed just one run to win the game. Second basemen Craig Counsell, who my kids had nicknamed "Chicken Wing" because he held his elbow up high when he batted, was on third base.

We watched breathlessly at the wind up and the pitch. It was a hit! Craig ran home and scored the winning run. We won the World Series! The home team crowd of 67,000 fans went nuts; everyone cheering madly and jumping wildly about.

Tim came up and ran to my arms, pointing to the stadium clock. "Dad, look!" he screamed. "Chicken ran at midnight!"

The large stadium clock read twelve midnight. It was Craig, the "Chicken Man," who had scored the winning run at midnight. My adrenaline surge disappeared as if I had been zapped with a tranquilizer dart. The crowd disappeared. I was only aware of Mike and Tim as we held each other and bawled.

I wanted to call Amy. She knew how much the World Series meant to me. But I knew, she was there. I could feel it. She was there with us. Somehow, some way, that nonsensical phrase, "Chicken runs at midnight" had been a prophecy that now connected us to her. Knowing that Amy would be with Him, God provided us with a connection between our two worlds during that incredible moment. The boys and I hugged and cried and hugged and cried. No one else could begin to understand what it all meant to the three of us.

After all the celebrating had died down at around 3 a.m., I walked back to the locker room and got my briefcase. Opening it, I reached into a side pocket and pulled out the phone message I always carried with me. "Dear Dad, Chicken runs at midnight. Love, Amy."

"We did it Ames," I cried softly. "And you were with me."

— Rich Donnelly

Rich Donnelly is currently a coach with the Milwaukee Brewers. During the off season, he travels around the country as a Catholic motivational speaker. You can contact him by calling Tiffany Rodriguez at (561) 218-5739.

See pictures related to this story at www.AmazingGraceOnLine.net/Heart

Of Angels and Strange Old Women in Manhattan

Years ago, when I lived in Manhattan, I knew a charismatic preacher on the Lower East Side. He had encountered a beggar near the Bowery one day and, like many who live in the city, was tempted to ignore the man. There are many homeless in New York City, and they can be a nuisance. Some are simply looking to buy drugs, so it is tempting to disregard them.

The preacher was ready to do just that but gave the beggar some money anyway. When he turned around the "bum" had disappeared. He was just *gone*. There was nothing to hide behind, and the preacher did not think there was any possibility he had walked away so quickly. Upon reflection, he came to believe this experience was a test from God, and that the beggar had been an angel.

I have no idea if his experience was supernatural, but many people report having such encounters. You probably have your own stories. I remember a friend who was out of work and looking for a job in midtown Manhattan. He did not know the preacher (my friend was not at all religious) but he too ran into what I can only describe as the "mysterious beggar." And like the preacher, my friend was also tempted to turn the homeless man away. Instead, something prompted him to give the guy $20 despite his own precarious financial situation. Soon after, my friend landed a job down on Wall Street. As he walked out of the place where he had just been hired, he spotted the same beggar—more than six miles south of the midtown location where he had seen him days before!

Was this beggar also an angel? According to
Hebrews 13:2, angels often come as "mysterious
strangers." I remember speaking with a woman from
Louisiana named Sondra Abrahams who had a near-
death experience. She said one of the most striking aspects
of her experience was learning from Christ how many
times in her life she had run into angels without knowing
it.

In the 1980s, shortly after my return to the Catholic
Church, I was walking down the east side of Third
Avenue one afternoon during rush hour. Suddenly an old
woman stood smack in front of me, stopping me in my
tracks. She faced me, standing right in my path. I had
never had anything quite like that happen before, and I
really do not remember many of her traits. I do remember
that she was short, perhaps a bit hunched over, like one of
the sweet elderly women who attended daily Mass at Our
Lady of Good Counsel around the corner.

She just stopped there, forced me to stop, faced me,
smiled, and made the sign of the cross. I will always
remember my feelings at that moment. She never said a
word; she just disappeared into the crowd. Later, while on
a business trip to Lewes, England, I was at early morning
Mass at a church dedicated to St. Michael. During the
exchange of peace, an elderly woman in front of me
turned with the same smile and sent a wave through me
of what I can only call grace as we shook hands. I could
not really say for sure, but I have wondered if it was the
same woman. Both acted in the same silent way.

On a later occasion, my sister told me she was in
Lower Manhattan—far from the Upper East Side—when
she ran into an elderly woman who made the sign of the

cross over her. I heard a similar story from a woman who worked in the publicity department at Doubleday Publishing who had an identical experience while riding the subway.

Was there some elderly woman running around New York blessing everyone, or are there angels in human form—even in the concrete jungles of Manhattan?

— Michael H. Brown

Michael Brown is an award-winning author whose work has appeared in such publications as the New York Times, Atlantic Monthly, Reader's Digest, *and* New York Magazine. *He has written thirteen Catholic books and six secular ones. Michael is the editor of SpiritDaily.com, a vibrant Catholic news site. He and his wife and three children live in Latham, New York.*

An Angel's Secret

Thirteen weeks pregnant with a much-wanted third child, I was putting in my last week of work in the hospital accounting office. An ultrasound three days earlier had revealed that my larger-than-usual size was not twins as suspected, but the result of a benign fibroid on my uterus.

"Nothing to worry about," I had been told. So why was Dr. Fields, my obstetrician, walking toward my desk with a look of deep concern? "Could you take a minute and come with me to my office?" he asked. "There's something I want to talk to you about." Although his office was just down the corridor, the tense silence that accompanied us turned the short walk into what seemed like a mile. Clearly, there was a problem.

If only my husband, Dan, could be with me now, I thought. He had been thrilled when he learned of the baby's late September due date. As a farmer in Linton, North Dakota, Dan would be finished harvesting by then, allowing him plenty of time to help with the new baby and our other two children, John, age four, and Renae, age two.

By the time we reached the office, my stomach churned with fear. The doctor held the ultrasound and circled the head region. By thirteen weeks the brain should be developing, he explained. Where there should have been gray-colored matter, instead, there were only black circles which indicated no brain development.

I was so scared, it was hard for me to even talk. I left my doctor's office after he scheduled a second ultrasound with a specialist who was coming from Bismarck the following week. At home that evening, unburdening myself to Dan brought some relief. We shared the fear and pain but also a firm resolve that whatever the outcome, God had given us this baby to love and care for.

The result of the second ultrasound was disheartening. Black circles showed clearly in the head region. "Bilateral frontal atrophy," was the scientific term, which meant there was no brain development. The specialist explained that women often miscarry in this situation but if not, the baby would probably not survive long after birth, not more than six months.

Termination of the pregnancy was presented as an option by the doctor. We responded immediately that this was not an option for us. The baby would live or die according to God's plan.

We kept asking God for a healthy baby, but now we also asked Him to give us strength for whatever happened. The first few weeks were emotionally agonizing. I couldn't sleep at night, I was so sad and scared. Would my baby live long enough to be baptized? Would he be born so severely handicapped that it would be difficult to care for my other children?"

Gradually, through prayer, fear evolved into acceptance. I began praying, "God, I know You will take care of this child. And if I cannot be my baby's mother on earth, the Blessed Mother will be his mother in heaven."

~

A month before the baby's due date, I arrived at the doctor's office for another ultrasound. Watching my baby kick and wiggle on the screen, I was unexpectedly filled with joy. It was as if an angel had come down from heaven and let me know he would be okay.

If an angel had told me a secret, the doctors were not let in on it. The test showed minimal brain development—enough that the baby had a chance of surviving—but he was expected to be profoundly mentally disabled. I was informed that at birth, the baby would probably not even cry, being incapable of responding to the birth experience in a normal way.

Undeterred by scientific reality, I went home ecstatic. "I'm going to have a baby!" I kept thinking over and over. I had gone from my initial paralyzing fear to acceptance to jubilation at the coming of our baby. My enthusiasm rubbed off on Dan, but still he was cautious. I knew my feelings did not make sense, but I felt so sure that our baby was going to be fine.

The night before I went into labor, Dan and I held hands with our two children and prayed together before an outdoor shrine of the Holy Family that Dan's parents had built on the farmland where they themselves raised twelve children. I lit two candles and left them burning there.

At 2 a.m., I went into labor. I called my doctor who told me to make the one-hour drive into Bismarck's St. Alexius hospital where he and other specialists would be waiting. On the way to the hospital, I looked out the car window and noticed my candles still burning. I felt a warm glow in my heart and instinctively made the sign of the cross. Dan looked over at me, smiled, and said, "Everything is going to be all right."

I was greeted at the hospital by my doctor, a delivery room nurse, two extra nurses and a neonatal specialist who were all prepared for a baby expected to struggle with life. After a short labor, baby Robert entered the world with a loud, healthy wail. Everyone was shocked. This little guy was not supposed to realize he had just been born. His piercing screams continued until he was placed into my arms. Then little Robert immediately quieted and gazed into my eyes. When he did that, I was the one who cried.

The medical personnel watched awestruck as Dan and I cooed over our new son. After a short while, Robert was taken for the standard APGAR testing. He passed with flying colors. The specialist did an ultrasound on his brain and announced with disbelief, "This baby is fine." Handing him back to me he added, "We're not going to do any more tests." By now even the nurses were crying.

Dr. Fields said he could offer no explanation as to how three ultrasounds indicated there was little or no brain development and instead a healthy baby was born. Because three separate readings analyzed by several experts all pointed to the same conclusion, he said it seems impossible that any errors were made.

Dan and I are convinced that our little boy's health is a miracle, a true gift from God. Today, at eight years old, Robert is perfectly healthy. Not a day goes by that I do not realize how blessed we are.

— Marie Vetter

Dan and Marie Vetter own and operate a farm of small grains and cow/calf pairs. They have four children, John, Renae, Robert, and Katherine. Marie is the secretary/bookkeeper for her parish and is the youth leader for the Catholic Order of Foresters.

See pictures related to this story at www.AmazingGraceOnLine.net/Heart

Emergency Road Service

Sitting behind a long line of cars on the Pennsylvania Turnpike, I could not believe what was happening. There was a roadblock just a couple miles ahead of me, which meant I had come within five minutes of completely missing the traffic jam. "So much for getting an early start," I thought, turning off my car engine.

I was the guest speaker for "Theology on Tap–NYC," an evening seminar for young adults in New York City. Although I knew that I only needed two hours to get from my home in Philadelphia to New York, I had left five hours early to ensure arriving in plenty of time.

Getting stuck in traffic was more frustrating than worrisome at that point. I still have another four hours, I thought to myself. "It shouldn't be a problem," I said to my friend Jim, who was driving with me to the seminar. But as time moved forward and traffic did not, I became concerned. I called the conference planners every hour to let them know of my situation.

When 5 p.m. arrived and there was still no sign of movement, making it in time for the scheduled 7 p.m. talk was beginning to look impossible. If traffic did not start moving within minutes, I would have to put in the call to cancel the talk. I felt totally helpless. There was nothing I could do, except ...

"We need to pray," I said. It was our only hope. We immediately began praying the Rosary. Within one minute after our final "amen" we saw a car going the *opposite* direction on the shoulder of the road right next to us. It is illegal to drive on the shoulder, even if you are going in the same direction as the rest of traffic, let alone in the opposite direction. But several cars started turning around the tightly cramped highway and heading down the shoulder in the opposite direction.

"Something's going on," I said to Jim.

Suddenly, for the first time a possible way out had presented itself. I immediately turned the car around and headed down the same shoulder.

Just a hundred yards behind us was a makeshift exit the police had set up through someone's back yard. Using back roads we found our way back onto the Turnpike and sped our way up to New York. We made it to the conference with fifteen minutes to spare.

I do not know whether our prayer had started the chain of events that led to this traffic jam escape, but it showed me yet again the power of God's grace. When situations look hopeless, we are never helpless.

— Matthew Pinto

Matthew Pinto is co-editor of the Amazing Grace *series. His biography appears at the end of the book.*

Spot the Monk

If a picture is worth a thousand words, what do you suppose a video image is worth? What about a video image of our Lord Jesus Christ in the Blessed Sacrament?

I oversee our religious community's web site. I had the idea to provide a live image of our Eucharistic Adoration chapel, which is uploaded every minute twenty-four hours a day, seven days a week so the web cam can bring Jesus closer to people through their computers. I quickly learned that this image was indeed worth much more than a thousand words.

I have received e-mails from homebound people who praise the web cam as a great comfort when they cannot get to church. People with insomnia have written to say they use it during long nights when sleep eludes them. Others use it as a home oratory where the family can gather in prayer. One psychiatrist uses it to pray with her patients during treatment.

This feedback confirmed to me that the web cam was the next best thing to being there. But there was one use that I never could have imagined—a game. Since some of our monks occasionally pass in front of the camera for a moment, a group of office workers turned this cyber image into the "Spot the Monk" game.

A non-Catholic named Richard wrote to tell me about it: "Brother John, in my quest to see a monk on your monk-cam, I have set up a web ring of a few friends of mine to watch the monk-cam at most hours of the day. This is the exciting part: Sarah saw a monk! I was not fortunate enough to lay eyes on him, but I know you guys are out there! Thank you for putting your web cam up. We love it!"

I must admit, I never envisioned the "Spot the Monk" game, but neither did I envision what would follow. Because of this game, Richard started reading articles on our web site. In his next email to me, he wanted information about becoming Catholic. I directed him to a Catholic parish and sent him the *Catechism of the Catholic Church*. Richard eventually was received into the Catholic Church. Now, he tries to attend adoration daily at his local parish.

Little did Richard realize that by trying to spot a monk, he would find Jesus. Now that is a game worth playing.

— Br. John Raymond

Brother Raymond is a founder of the Monks of Adoration. His website, featuring the live video cam of the Blessed Sacrament, can be reached at www.MonksofAdoration.com.

See pictures related to this story at www.AmazingGraceOnLine.net/Heart

Chapter 2

Family Matters

Random Acts of "Kidness"

My eleven-year-old daughter and I were recently in a huge chain store. She headed over to the school supply section while I went for groceries. I finished shopping before she did and was standing in line at one of the fifteen checkouts. Her view of me was blocked by a huge book display. As I had plenty of time to spare, I watched her observing a bewildered elderly man shuffle around the front counter area. The poor soul had on shower slippers and clothing that had seen much better days. It was obvious that he was homeless.

I saw the sad look on Amanda's face as she scrabbled around in her small purse. I knew what she was doing, and had to restrain myself from giving her the money to give to the gentleman. She wanted to use her own money, so I squashed my motherly instincts. She left her cart in line, and walked a short distance behind the man, where she dropped the rolled up one dollar bills to the floor. My heart and eyes filled as she gently tapped him on the shoulder and pointed the money out to him. As he joyfully scooped up the money, I could read his lips telling Amanda "God bless you." My daughter sweetly shook her head no. She smiled up at him, said a few words, and then skipped back to her cart.

I pretended to be busy with my checkbook as I quickly wiped my eyes. Once back in our car and heading home, Amanda shyly related the story of how she had noticed the man looking at the cookies in the store. He had counted the change in his pocket then put the cookies he wanted to buy back on the shelf. She said, "Mom, I knew he was hungry and he seemed sort of confused. I didn't want him to be hungry."

"So, did you give him some money or buy him some food?" I asked her.

My little angel replied, "No, Mama. I didn't want him to be embarrassed that I thought he was poor, so I told him I found some money on the floor, and that I thought it was his. He said, 'God bless you,' and I really do feel blessed. Then I showed him the bananas on sale."

This little "random act of 'kidness'" from my own child will continue to bless me for many years to come.

— Angie Ledbetter

Angie Ledbetter is a freelance writer, author, and columnist. Her latest work, a co-authored Catholic book, Seeds of Faith ~ An Inspirational Almanac, *can be found at www.SeedsOfFaithAlmanac.com. In addition to being a writer and editor, Angie is a wife, mom of three, an involved Scouter, and devoted ministry worker. To read more of Angie's work, visit her personal writing site, www.GumboWriter.com.*

Billy: A Family Story

Billy Lutter tumbled to the wooden floor of his home. His parents picked him up and tried again to help him walk. It was no use. This was 1939, and doctors had been telling the Lutters to institutionalize five-year-old Billy for some time, a common recommendation then for children with physical and mental disabilities. Billy's parents, a steel-worker and a homemaker, struggled with the decision to send Billy away.

"This was back in the Depression," says Fred Lutter, Billy's older brother by two years. "Things were tough all around. It was a very tearful situation." Their hearts breaking, the Lutters drove Billy from their home outside Chicago to a state facility 200 miles away. They visited regularly for a year. But administrators, worried that such meetings might upset the other residents, advised them to stop coming.

"My brother realized who his parents were," Fred says. "To be left like that was very traumatic. I felt very sad to see my parents in such turmoil."

The years rolled by. Billy's siblings got married and had their own children. Everybody thought about Billy, but his name was not spoken. Billy's parents grew old and, as they aged, grew infirm. They had done what they thought was best for Billy, but his absence had left a gaping, raw wound for the family.

The Lutters' sad story inadvertently took a happier turn thirty-five years later. It began when Julie Hess signed up her six-year-old daughter Jenny, who had

Down Syndrome, for a religious-education program for the disabled. Sadly, Jenny never had a chance to take a class. She died shortly afterward.

Julie Hess nevertheless went on to volunteer with the program that she had hoped her daughter might enjoy. By 1987, she had become a full-time employee of the Archdiocese of Chicago's Special Religious Education Division.

One of Julie's favorite students was an easygoing older man with a white mustache and gray hair. His records labeled him mildly retarded. He suffered from cerebral palsy and needed a walker to get around. His hearing was bad, but he knew a bit of sign language.

Despite his circumstances, Bill had a special spark. Though he could only say a handful of words, he was a good communicator. And he radiated cheerfulness. Bill was especially religious. He wore a cross around his neck and enjoyed being in church. He took part enthusiastically in the sacraments.

"He's very prayerful," Julie says. "He has a deep sense of the sacred. God is a presence in his life, bringing him peace and a reason to hope."

Bill grew very animated when Julie talked about family, so she decided to find at least one member of his family. But the group home told her that Bill had no family. Even still, Julie was determined. As the years passed, she took up Bill's cause with renewed passion. Finally, in 1993, an administrator gave Julie a name and phone number. The suburban number was for Kathy Dever, Bill's sister.

Only brother Fred was old enough to have memories of Billy. His sisters, Kathy and Bonnie, knew next to nothing. "My brother said he was a vegetable," Kathy says, "and that it was best that we didn't see him. You have to understand the times. People ask us, 'How could your parents give him up?' There was no schooling like there is today. No way would they do the same thing today. But things are different now."

As time went by, Fred thought more and more about Billy. What was he like? Was it possible to bring him back to the family? It was the fear of the unknown, not knowing what to expect, that kept Fred from initiating contact.

It was decided that Fred would meet with Billy first. On the day of the meetings, Fred brought a photo of their mother. Bill studied the photo. Julie Hess realized the challenge. "Bill understands family," she says. "But how do we get him to understand this is his mother?"

Julie put the photo on Bill's chest and pointed at him. "His face suddenly changed and lit up like a light bulb," Julie recalls. "He nodded and got excited."

The next challenge was to help Bill understand that Fred was his brother. Julie put the photo by Bill and signed "mother" and placed the photo by Fred and signed "mother." An amazed look rushed over his face.

"Bud," Bill said.

Fred nearly fell off the chair. "That's what he called me when he was little," Fred said.

That night, Fred called his sister Kathy. "I just met my brother," Fred sobbed.

Bill's sisters visited two weeks later and then it was time for Bill to meet his mother. It happened on Mother's Day in the church basement, where they embraced for the first time in fifty years.

Until she died three years later, mother and son were inseparable, at least emotionally. "They saw each other,

held hands and never let go, at least figuratively," says
Hess. "She was so happy when they were together." Fred
says that Bill filled a big hole in their mother's life. "She
felt so relieved to have her family back again," he adds.

Bill now spends his weekends and holidays with his family. He has bonded with his great-nephews and great-
nieces. "He loves kids," says Kathy.

Not long ago, Bill visited Fred in Florida, where the
elder brother has retired. Being near the clouds on the
plane ride stirred his religious feelings. "He pointed at the
clouds and made the sign of the cross," Kathy says. "He
thought we were up by Jesus."

The Lutter family has since moved Bill into a more
pleasant group home in a suburb closer to his sisters.
"This has changed his life entirely," Julie says. "He held
on to the memories of his family for his whole life, and
now they've become real."

— Jay Copp

Jay Copp's biography appears after the story Inspired by a Martyr *in
Chapter One.*

Falling for Jesus

It was Lent and I had recently been to confession. My penance was to pray the Stations of the Cross. At the time, I had three little ones ages four and younger, and I was largely pregnant with my fourth.

I did not know how I was going to keep them all quiet. Praying the Stations of the Cross would be an ordeal with all of them tagging along. I decided to pray the stations at the National Shrine of Our Lady of Czestochowa in Doylestown, Pennsylvania, where there is an outdoor Stations of the Cross in a semi-circle on a sloped hill. At least the kids could be outside, I thought.

Since the route of the Stations was paved, I brought the youngest in a stroller and the two older girls walked beside me. I started at the beginning, but before long my children were running circles around the stations, playing a game of tag. I was dismayed at their lack of piety and involvement. With a sigh and several warnings to be careful, I had reached the station where Jesus falls for the first time. Isabel, my three-year-old, ran behind the station, tripped, and fell. She dusted herself off and continued to play. After making sure there were no scraped knees or tears, I moved on to the next station. I tried to engage my daughter, Veronica, then four, by pointing out her name on the station where Veronica wipes the face of Jesus. But she quickly lost interest. I resigned myself to the fact that they were just not going to pay attention.

I reached the station where Jesus falls for the second time and began the prayer. Isabel ran behind the station, tripped, and fell again.

"Isabel Eve! Would you stop that?" I scolded her. "I've already told you to be careful. Because you didn't listen you have fallen for the second time."

Veronica looked up at the station before her and pointing to it she announced: "Just like Jesus!"

— Victoria Gisondi

Victoria Gisondi is the daughter of Cuban refugees and the proud mother of four children, three girls and a boy, all under the age of six. Victoria loves to read and spends a lot of time reading to her children. She and her family live near Philadelphia, in Chalfont, Pennsylvania.

See pictures related to this story at www.AmazingGraceOnLine.net/Heart

Duffy's Rose

Mama never forgot her "other" son.

Mama kept the items that meant something special in a box labeled "Fanny Farmer Choice Candies." Among them, placed there long ago, were the mummified remains of a single rose, now as hard as a rock and showing only the barest hint of color on the top of one tight petal.

The rose had been a gift to Mama from a special boy named Duffy shortly before he went off to war. Duffy was my brother Kevin's best friend, whom we all had sort of "adopted."

His real name was Dorian Fitzhugh. Duffy's mother, Megan Fitzhugh, died in the labor that gave him life. Consequently, Duffy's dad, Red Hugh, drifted in a world of grief and eventually sent the boy to live with an aunt in Pennsylvania. But when the aunt became ill during his eighth-grade year, young Dorian returned to our city.

At that point, Kevin sought to make his newfound, silent, and somewhat morose friend a part of our life. Giving him the nickname "Duffy" was one step in that direction.

As the two grew in friendship, sharing unparalleled skills as athletes, their kindred spirits drew them even closer. In no time, Duffy became a part of the fabric of our lives. And considering Duffy's difficult upbringing, it was evident he appreciated the acceptance he found in our crowded home.

Over the years, I often heard nuns and priests at St. Columbkille comment on the friendship between Kevin and Duffy. On the athletic field or the basketball court, they were the ones to watch. They truly complemented one another: Kevin's outgoing and genuine laughter never quite overshadowing Duffy's more timid yet radiant smile.

One Sunday in May, though, as we Patricks remembered the day's primary occasion and hustle off to fetch Mama's gift, Duffy disappeared. His only good-bye was a comment that indicated he would be returning shortly.

"Happy Mother's Day, Mama!" we were soon calling while we carried our small gifts out to the oilcloth-covered table. "Happy Mother's Day!"

As she usually did, Mama feigned surprise and wiped her hands on her apron. "Oh my! What's all this? You'd think it was a birthday or something!" The ritual was the same, year after year. But we liked it, and Mama never seemed to tire of it either.

Carefully, Mama unwrapped the gifts: a lace-bordered handkerchief and a pair of tickets to "Bank Night" at the Pearl Theatre. Now she and Mrs. O'Malley could go without worrying over money. And here was a jar of quince jelly, too—her favorite—with a promise it would be safe in the icebox, left for only her consumption. One by one, the gifts were opened and the homemade cards read. Tommy had sent a card and long letter which Mama counted as precious as any other gifts.

Just as we were leaving the table, Duffy returned, walking through the door without needing to do any knocking. In one hand, he carried his baseball cleats for our weekly Sunday ritual, and in the other, a still-moist American Beauty rose.

"Here, Mrs. Patrick!" he beamed. "Happy Mother's Day!"

Mama took the rose and studied its subtle beauty. Though the flower was still in a fairly tight bud, dew glistened on one velvet petal. Its stem was long and green, with sparkling leaves touched with traces of moisture. Even in the crowded room, the rose's potent fragrance danced sweetly among us.

A pause in our boisterous conversation ensued as we watched Kevin's best friend standing there, his hand still outstretched toward Mama. Thinking back, remembering, I can still see her face. First she gazed on the rose, and then she turned her eyes to the boy who had brought it to her.

"Thank you, Dorian!" Mama said with obvious affection. "Thank you, indeed!"

She motioned for Duffy to lean toward her, and she kissed him as she would one of us.

"Just thought you should have it," Duffy said, blushing self-consciously.

But the drama of the moment was fleeting. With the first good sun of the season and a balmy breeze tempting us, we soon hurried out to offer up our first ball game to the waiting spring. When we returned home that night, Duffy's rose sat beneath the picture of the Sacred Heart in Mama's treasured bud vase, which had once belonged to her own mother in Ireland.

"Lettin' Jesus share your rose, Mama?" Kevin laughed. Mama just nodded and smiled.

Gradually, in the days that followed, the rose opened to its full glory. For a long time, we thought Mama had simply thrown it away when its beauty had begun to wane. But three years later, we were to learn differently.

Shortly after graduation from Holy Redeemer, Duffy died in combat in the rice paddies of North Korea. The news struck all of us, especially Kevin, with a blow from which we never really recovered. To be sure, in spite of the passage of more than forty years, Kevin will even now sit alone from time to time and remember his friend. But one aspect of our caring for Duff nearly escaped us in our grief over his untimely death.

Following Duffy's military funeral and interment in the little cemetery behind the church, a get-together was held in the parish hall. When we later returned to the stillness of our apartment to mourn our loss in silence, Tommy, who was home on a furlough, cautioned Danny and me to respect Kevin's inner grief and let him work it out for himself.

Though we all suffered that evening, we learned Kevin was not the only one affected so greatly. As we sat there, David turned on the radio, keeping the sound low. John, Mama's pet canary, chirped hesitantly before lapsing into a respectful silence as if he, too, felt the sense of loss pervading our home.

As the rest of us shared stories of Duffy's life, Mama got up from her chair and disappeared into her bedroom. Moments later, she returned carrying the white candy-box repository containing her earthly treasures.

Then, carefully lifting the rose out of the box, Mama held up the blackened remains of that long-ago Mother's Day. She had cut the stem short so it would fit in the box, but a few leaves remained along with a wealth of dried thorns which had steadfastly weathered the years.

"I pricked my finger," she said softly, "the day Dorian gave this to me. Pricked it on this very thorn when I went to put it in the vase for Jesus to share."

Tapping lightly on the still sharp thorn, she quietly continued. "Dorian had so little in the way of joy when he came among us," she sighed. "Ah! I often wished I could take away that boy's sorrows."

I studied Mama. It was not like her to talk this way. Nor had I ever seen her talk on while tears rolled down her cheeks.

"He gave me this rose," Mama said, "and I kissed his cheek. Then, when you boys were getting ready for your ball game, he sat down beside me to wait. He gently put his hand in mine and he thanked me for being his mother."

Until that moment, we had never known of the touching exchange.

"Ah!" she uttered from the depths of her own grief. "He's got his own mother as well as Mother Mary with him now. But, for a while, he was like another of my own, and I'll miss him so much!" With that, Mama put the rose back in the box, carried it back to her room, and shut the door. We knew she would grieve in her own privacy, so we let her be.

— Sean Patrick

Sean Patrick is a professional writer, retired from a lifetime in law enforcement. For the past sixteen years, Sean has been a columnist for Catholic Digest. *His work has also appeared in such publications as* The Family, Our Family, the Ligourian, *and* The Priest. *Sean is the author of three books:* Patrick's Corner, Kingdom of the Flies, *and* The Best of Sean Patrick. *He and his wife live in rural Ohio in the midst of the Old Order Amish.*

See pictures related to this story at www.AmazingGraceOnLine.net/Heart

It's For the Birds

One evening I listened to a robin's repetitive song with my young son, Thomas. The sun was setting and it seemed to me that the robin's soulful chirps were destined for heaven.

Looking out the window together I explained: "That's how birds pray to God." Thomas listened another moment to the unending repetitive song and earnestly replied, "Well then, Mom, that bird must be praying the Rosary."

— Jane Seifert

Jane Seifert and her husband, Mike, have been married for eighteen years. They have three children, ages seventeen, fourteen, and ten. Jane is very proud of her kids and considers herself their number one fan. She and her family live in Bismarck, North Dakota.

Mama's Wish

What I remember most about my grandfather's funeral is the pained look in my mother's eyes. It was not just the grief over her father's death that I saw, but also the sadness because my sister, brother, and I could not receive Holy Communion. Before Mass she told us, "I asked Sister if you could receive communion just this once because it is a special circumstance—your grandfather's funeral—but she told me no. You will have to go to confession before you may receive again."

I grew up in a strong Catholic home. I had fond memories of saying my prayers with Mama. My parents were very involved in our parish and went to church every Sunday and Holy Days without fail. Daddy made sure we always arrived at least thirty minutes early for Mass. In his mind, if we were not early, we were late. Mass was not just something to get over with, according to him. He felt it was important to spend some time with God, praying and meditating before Mass began. At that time, I never questioned their faith; I went along. I even belonged to a youth group as a teenager and actually enjoyed it.

Although I never rejected the faith of my youth, as I grew older and went to college, I took advantage of my newfound independence. I was an adult and no one could tell me what to do now. Not only did I no longer have to arrive thirty minutes early to Mass, I did not have to go at all.

Looking back, I am not completely sure what I thought. I never rejected God or the Catholic faith, I was just apathetic. I thought I was a good person and it was not necessary to follow a bunch of rules like going to Mass every Sunday. In reality, I think I filled my life up with so many other things like parties, socializing, shopping and the like, that God was pushed far down on my list of priorities. I knew He deserved more attention than I was giving Him, but I felt there would be time enough for that one day.

～

The fact that I could not receive Communion at my grandfather's funeral Mass did not bother me at all, but it was my mother's disappointment that had touched me. Still, at twenty-three, with a husband and a three-year-old daughter, it was easy for me to block out the whole incident and get on with my life. But only three weeks later came news of another death in my family—my mother's.

Mama had been in a car accident. I was called immediately and the family rushed to the hospital. But it was too late. Mama had died at the scene of the accident. She was only forty-eight. I was in shock—it had happened so suddenly. And yet, there was an element of peace. Mama had been such a faithful Catholic and good person, surely she was ready to meet God.

At Mama's funeral Mass, I again had to face the fact that the Church did not allow me to receive Communion. I had been away for so long, I needed to go to confession before I could receive. To do so otherwise would be a sacrilege. This time, sitting out during Communion was not as easy as it had been just three weeks earlier. Here I was at Mama's funeral and I could not fulfill what I knew had been her greatest wish for me; to be a part of the Church and receive Jesus in the Eucharist.

I had ignored my mother's gentle proddings while she was alive, but now, from the next world, I heard her loud and clear. There was no returning to my life as it had been. Oh, I tried, but Mama would have none of it. God surely had given her a microphone now. The unsettled feeling that I had put God off long enough overcame me. I knew I had to return to the sacraments for my mother, for my daughter and mostly for myself. After ten years away from confession, I went and gave the priest an earful; going all the way back to my high school days.

It felt so good to be home again on Sundays and part of God's Church again. I was where I should have been all along. "Now that I am where Mama always wished me to be, I'm going to strive to be the person God wants me to be," I thought. To my joy, my husband joined the Catholic Church two years later.

Seven years and four more children later, I can see the fruits of practicing our faith. I was too hard headed to see it while Mama was alive but in her death, she finally got through to me. Thank you, Mama!

— Gwen DeLaune

Gwen DeLaune writes from the Jambalaya capital of the world—Gonzales, Louisiana. Her husband, Tommy, has the enviable skill of being able to cook enough Jambalaya to feed four hundred people at once! Gwen is a stay-at-home mom of five children, including two-year-old twins. She loves to go to the park and read with her kids, as well as help out with the youth group at her parish.

See pictures related to this story at www.AmazingGraceOnLine.net/Heart

Healing Grace

Mother and I had never been close. She was very tempera-mental and domineering. Her quick temper had inflicted great emotional wounds on our family as we were grow-ing up. My father, on the other hand, was a gentle soul. I adored him and was always Daddy's little girl.

As an adult I tried to leave the past in the past, but my mother's behavior while my beloved father was dying brought fresh strain to our relationship. Mother was nei-ther patient nor kind during Dad's suffering. The disrup-tion in her life angered her, and probably scared her. Yet, I could not accept her bad temperament during this time.

After my father's death in 1985, however, I knew I had a responsibility to both God and Dad to forgive. It helped to remember how patient my father had always been. He loved my mother, faults and all. I recalled many times as a child that whenever Mom had been especially cruel, my father would come into my room, out of my mother's earshot. He would hug me and say, "Please don't hate her; she needs more love and forgiveness than most people do. She is God's treasure just as you are."

After Dad's death, I wanted to honor my Dad. I knew his hopes and prayers were that I could love and forgive my mom. This was beyond my human frailties so I prayed to God for the grace to do so. As the years passed my feel-ings of distrust and resentment ebbed. I managed to lay the past to rest as Christ would have me do. Mother and I built a decent, if not perfect, relationship as mother and daughter. The past was just that—the past. The future I would leave to God.

Then, during the first week of September 1992, I awoke from a dream sensing a very firm command: "Go home and see your mother." I had ceased to question God's inspiration when I felt prompted by the Holy Spirit. As soon as daylight broke, I packed my suitcase. My husband suggested we call to make sure she was all right. Everything was fine and Mother sounded very happy that I would be visiting over Labor Day.

I arrived by mid-afternoon and Mom and I had an enjoyable time going out to dinner and visiting friends. Mother cut the evening short explaining there was a program on television she wanted to watch. When we got home I got ready for bed and sat in the living room reading my nightly scripture as Mom watched TV. The television volume gradually increased. Every few moments Mom asked, "Does that bother you?"

"No, it's fine," I repeatedly told her.

Finally she had turned the volume all the way up. "Does that bother you?" She asked in a loud but shaky voice. I put down the Bible and looked at her.

"Well, it is loud. Are you trying to tell me something? Are you having hearing problems?" I asked.

Mother looked at me with searching eyes. Still, I did not understand. Returning the sound back to normal, she explained. "No, what I mean is, does this program bother you?" For the first time, I looked over to see what she was watching. It was a program on child abuse. "I was not talking about the sound," she said. "I meant, what do you think of parents who abuse their children?"

I was caught off guard. I stared into her eyes. For the first time I recognized pain and remorse. Huge tears trickled down her cheeks. My response was instinctive.

"Mom, I love you," I cried, truly meaning it. "And if you are asking for my forgiveness, you have had it for years. Don't cry," I said, coming over to kiss her cheek. "It is all in the past. It doesn't matter any more." I then hugged her and wiped her tears away. No more words were needed. It truly was now in the past. For my proud mother to humble herself to ask forgiveness was a grace I never imagined.

The next day, Saturday, we began with a visit to church to pray the Rosary. Tears of joy and also of sorrow for all the wasted years streamed down my face. But I praised God for this new beginning. The rest of the day we filled with shopping and sharing as a mother and daughter who fully loved and respected one another. We went to an estate sale and found ourselves giggling and laughing like young school girls. Mom bought me a statue of Our Lady of the Immaculate Heart, which had seen better days. The face was chipped and it had no nose. But it was a precious treasure, representing our newfound love for one another. I basked in the grace of our healing. Surely this was why God called me home ... or so I thought. It turned out to be only the beginning.

On Sunday, we planned to attend a late morning Mass. Mom excused herself from our talk and laughter to make coffee, which she herself did not drink. Trying to make it on the stove with a whole cup of grounds in a small pot, she boiled it to the strength of turpentine. We ended up laughing until our sides hurt. We determined Mom's specialty—tea—would be a better choice.

While she boiled the water, I went to finish getting ready for Mass. All was right with the world. My heart sang. What a grace-filled day this would be!

As I came out of the bedroom, Mom came towards me from the kitchen. Her face looked stricken and blood-drained. "Christy, I feel so sick," she gasped. Suddenly, she began to vomit over and over. I grabbed hold of a wastepaper basket and held her head over it. Finally, she seemed to collapse in my arms. I felt her pulse racing. Her skin was cold and clammy. I called an ambulance.

Initially, Mom's ulcer was suspected, but the symptoms worsened. During the night, she suffered a stroke. Hours later, mom suffered an aneurysm requiring surgery. The doctors put her chance of survival at 25 percent. Then blood clots formed in both legs and she was rushed immediately back into surgery. There were too many clots and gangrene ensued. By the following week one of mom's legs had to be amputated. By the following year, the other leg was also removed.

The seeds of our new relationship blossomed into a solid bond as we prayed together through this hardship. It was not always easy for either of us. At first, Mom begged the doctors to just let her die rather than go through life with no legs. But before my eyes, I saw her begin to stretch her faith farther than she probably ever imagined it would need to go. On a daily basis I watched her let go and trust God.

In the grueling months following her amputation, she amazed everyone. The doctors said she would never be able to walk with prosthesis; she did. No one thought she was capable of managing with two artificial limbs. Mom again worked doggedly until she was able to walk unaided.

Mom was determined to return to her old life of independence. She was only partially successful. You see, she returned to independence, but it was not her old life. Instead, Mom grew to embrace a new life of acceptance and even joy. I watched in awe as she continually reached out to other suffering souls and ignited sparks of courage and love in their lives. Some people are never the same after experiencing a disability. In my mother's case, this was true in a good way. Her capacity to love seemed to grow and spread it to others.

Almost four years after her stroke, she got breast cancer and lived only another four months. It was but another cross she accepted and used to make a difference in the life of others by her example of joyfully accepting God's will. God's healing grace truly worked wonders in her life. I am so thankful I did not miss out on sharing it with her.

— Christine Trollinger

Christine Trollinger has contributed several wonderful stories to this book. You'll find her biography after The Badge of Grace *in Chapter One.*

A Valentine for Jesus (Almost)

Sometimes we get a glimpse of ourselves through our children. We aspire to do great things for God but then, oops, we don't quite hit the mark.

It was St. Valentine's Day and our oldest daughter, Buffy, who was then in third grade, came home from school with a few candies to share with her three younger siblings. I was in the kitchen preparing dinner when four-year-old John-Paul came in holding up a small pink candy heart.

With love in his eyes he announced, "Mommy, I'm going to give my heart to Jesus." I was delighted by our son's selfless devotion to Christ and praised him for it. He left the room smiling. Moments later he returned without the smile.

"Mommy," John-Paul said holding up the candy heart with a little nibble out of it, "I'm going to give Jesus this much of my heart." He waited anxiously for my response.

I continued to encourage him. "Son, Jesus will be delighted to share your heart with you," I gushed. A smile again graced his face as he returned to tell the other children, "See, God isn't mad at me!"

Satisfied that all was well, I returned to my task of making gravy. Suddenly there was John Paul again, tugging my slacks from behind. Once again my young son looked up at me with sad blue eyes but this time there was nothing in his hands.

"Mommy," he announced earnestly, "I don't think Jesus likes pink."

— Nellie Edwards

Nellie Edwards is the owner of a unique family business appropriately named "Mother of Eight Designs" in honor of her eight children. Six of the eight Edwards kids assist Nellie in hand casting and hand painting the religious and general interest "Keepsake" pins, plagues, and ornaments she sculpts. When Nellie is not busy crafting designs, she enjoys writing. To learn more about Nellie and her work, email her at mo8@ndak.net.

See pictures related to this story at www.AmazingGraceOnLine.net/Heart

Praying by the Book

"Now that I can read, Mom, can I have a
prayer book so I won't have to ad lib?"

The Negotiation

"Now about the events that led up to
the window incident ... "

Mother's Escort

Although Mother raised two children during the fifties and sixties, there was another child she could never forget. Mark was a beautiful red-headed baby who entered the world a month prematurely. He struggled to breathe from the beginning. Six hours after his birth, he gasped his last breath.

One of Mother's greatest regrets was never having held her baby son while he was alive. She was still in the hospital on the day of Mark's funeral, so my dad carried the little coffin into her hospital room for her to say good-bye. A mother can never forget the love of her child, and so it was with my mother. She got on with her life, but when people asked her how many children she had, she usually answered "three." So as teenagers, when my brother and I bought her a mother's ring, we made sure there were three stones surrounding her ruby birthstone; two "diamonds," to represent the April birthdays of her living children and the "aquamarine" for Mark's March birthday.

When my mother was ninety-four, she broke her hip. She stayed in the hospital three weeks, but then returned home, living independently by late April. In early May, she called me one day, her voice full of joy.

"Margaret, when I woke up this morning, there was a tall, handsome, red-haired man standing beside my bed," she said. "I was immediately flooded with peace and joy. I knew instantly that it was Mark. He told me, 'It won't be long. I will be coming for you.'" She repeated the story to my brother a few weeks later while they visited Mark's grave at the cemetery on Memorial Day.

Mother steadily improved, and I forgot about Mark's visit. Mother, however, started putting her affairs in order, wanting to sell her rental property, emptying closets, and repeatedly saying she wanted to clean out her house and have a rummage sale.

In mid-August, Mother fell and needed hospitalization; in early September she experienced a stroke. When she could not speak, she would often gaze upon the mother's ring we had given her. On December 8, the Feast of the Immaculate Conception, she was humming "Joy to the World" with some carolers as she sat eating supper at 6 p.m. Within the hour, she had passed away.

The next day at the funeral home, the funeral director handed me a small black bag containing Mother's jewelry. As I opened the bag and her Mother's ring fell into my hand, all at once I remembered Mother's visitor. I realized Mark had come for her. It was a comfort to know she did not leave this world alone.

— Margaret Sitte

Margaret Sitte is currently enjoying her freshman year as a North Dakota state legislator. She is the happy mother of four and former schoolteacher of eight years. Margaret is also a freelance writer, previously serving as an editorial-page columnist for the Bismarck Tribune. *Her work has been featured in* Home & Away *and* Our Sunday Visitor. *For twenty years, she lived only four blocks from her mother.*

See pictures related to this story at www.AmazingGraceOnLine.net/Heart

Quacks, Cracks, and Snacks

"Dad, can I just peek inside?" our ten-year-old son Luke asked, holding a cardboard box.

"Wait until we get home," my husband, Mark, answered. "I don't want ducklings flopping around the car."

This was a day Luke had dreamed of for weeks. Finally, ducks! We had moved out into the country two months earlier. Even though we had dogs, cats, and assorted reptiles and amphibians, Luke was impatient for some kind of farm animal. His five brothers and sisters were mildly interested in the ducklings, but not like Luke was. He was the one who had pleaded mercilessly for them.

Even though Luke had begged us for the ducks, it was the grasshoppers that clinched it. There was a serious invasion of them that summer of 1996, inflicting major damage on Mark's first country garden.

"They eat grasshoppers?" Mark had asked with sudden interest. That's when Luke knew his dad would relent.

Luke barely waited until the engine turned off before he bounced out of the car with his box. As if unwrapping a precious treasure, Luke gingerly lifted the lid. One by one the ducklings jumped out into a blinding August sun. Never content just to watch critters, he cornered and scooped up the ducklings one by one. As he held them securely and talked softly, each one relaxed in his hand until he slowly put it down and lifted another.

"I'm going to name this one Quacks," Luke decided, holding the littlest one. As Quacks calmed down, Luke held him gently against his chest and stroked his fluffy down.

The remainder of the day was spent with my kids and neighbors coming in and out of the yard to watch the peeping little flock. Luke never left the brood except to eat dinner. Throughout the day he herded them in and out of Mark's garden for several periods of grasshopper patrol.

As the sun began to set, Luke steered his ducklings into the garden for one last snack. When he attempted to return the flock to their pen, however, he accidentally stepped into their huddle and scattered them. The other ducks drew back together but Quacks ran off. Luke hurriedly got the flock into the pen and then chased Quacks where he had scampered behind a storage chest in the garage.

"Good, I've got him cornered," Luke thought. When he moved the chest aside, he heard little peeps but Quacks was nowhere in sight. Taking a closer look, Luke gasped. Quacks had fallen down a small drainage pipe. The opening was golf-ball sized. Luke ran into the house for a flashlight. The deep hole only swallowed up his light. Stricken, he walked into the house to find me.

"Mom, something bad has happened," Luke said. He explained the situation. "Is there anything we can do?" he asked doubtfully.

I went with him to the hole. "I can't think of anything," I told him helplessly.

"That's what I thought," he said and sadly turned to the house. "And he was my favorite one too—Quacks." The day which had started with such promise had turned sour. Bedtime was quiet except for the heartbreaking peeps that drifted into my second-floor bedroom from the garage underneath.

There were still eleven ducklings left but the little lost one broke our hearts. The parable of the Good Shepherd suddenly took on new relevance. Quack's frantic cries continued through the night. When I awoke to his peeps early the next morning, I wondered how long before lack of food and water would finally quiet him.

"Food," I thought. "That's it!" Luke, the first one up, was just coming out of his room. "Luke," I whispered, "I have an idea. What if you used a piece of fishing line and tied a grasshopper to the end of it? If Quacks is hungry enough, maybe he'll swallow it and you can pull him up. Then we can cut the end of the fishing line off." I admitted I had no idea if he could survive swallowing the fishing line.

"It's worth a try," Luke said, bounding out the door. He returned a short time later.

"Mom," Luke called excitedly. "Can you pray? Quacks bites the grasshopper but when I pull up the line he lets go."

I was surprised by the question. Pray for a duck? Luke looked at me hopefully, so of course I told him yes.

As he left to try again, Luke's request suddenly made perfect sense. God made animals with feelings. They got cold, scared, lonely, tired, and hungry. I sat down in the living room and prayed for God to guide Quacks up out of the hole. In minutes Luke returned with a big smile and a little duckling.

"He bit the grasshopper and I was able to pull him all the way up," he explained breathlessly. "When I grabbed him, he just let the grasshopper drop out of his mouth."

By now the other kids were coming downstairs. As we filled them in on the rescue, I couldn't get over the fact that Quacks had actually made it out of the hole.

"Didn't you all think it was impossible that we'd ever see Quacks again?" I asked.

The kids looked at me surprised. "I knew God could do anything so I prayed to Him last night to save Quacks," seven-year-old Tyler said, nonchalantly.

"That's what I did too," agreed Luke.

Now, I was really impressed. Their faith had no limits. If God could save wayward souls that fall through the cracks, how could I have doubted that He would be willing to save our wayward Quacks?

— Patti Maguire Armstrong

Patti Maguire Armstrong is co-editor of Amazing Grace for the Catholic Heart. *Her biography appears at the end of the book.*

See pictures related to this story at www.AmazingGraceOnLine.net/Heart

They Aren't So Smart

It was the spring of my daughter Molly's third-grade year. She was going through a series of tests to qualify for a once-a-week science program offered for gifted kids in our Anchorage, Alaska, school district. She had scored very high on standardized testing at the Catholic school she attended, St. Elizabeth's, so this further testing was suggested to my husband and me. After the second day of testing, the teacher came out shaking his head saying he had never tested a kid like this and that we should consider sending her to the gifted school.

I informed him Molly went to a Catholic school for her spiritual foundation and growth, which is more important to her future than her academic level. (We also felt she was getting a good education.) After leaving the school office, Molly wanted to know why the teacher talked about another school. I explained to her that it was a school for smart kids but that she would be staying at St. Elizabeth's because learning about God was more important. I explained that the other school taught children who were very intelligent but they did not teach them about God or start the day with a prayer. She looked immediately relieved (she loves St. Elizabeth's), but then a troubled look crossed her face.

"Mom," she said, "they can't be that smart over there if they don't teach about God."

— Mariann Petersen

Mariann Petersen lives in Anchorage, Alaska, with her two girls, Molly and Shannon, and husband, Sonny. She has happily retired from corporate life to raise her family and volunteer.

Midnight Run

"Remember how you looked forward
to having a son to take hikes with?"

Of Pirates and Priests

Surely the poem that asks what little boys are made of had my oldest son, Michael, in mind. "Frogs and snails and puppy dogs tails ... " as well as trucks and forts and pirates and swords; these things define his world.

Michael has always thrown himself into life, which my wife, Maryanne, and I make sure includes the spiritual. Early on, he learned the prayer to St. Michael (he's the angel who has a "fire sword", according to my son), and he could point out Jesus on the crucifix before he could talk. Our Blessed Mother Mary, the angels and saints, and the Church were as firmly planted in his world as Captain Hook and Power Rangers.

One Sunday, when Michael was nearly three, I carried him up with me in the Communion line. The priest happened to be wearing a patch due to a permanent eye problem he had. As I turned and walked down the aisle, Michael looked back over my shoulder at Father with big eyes. "Dad," he asked loudly, "is Father a pirate?"

Of course, I laughed, as did the nearby parishoners, but my heart also warmed. What an awesome blessing and incredible responsibility to form the spirit of our children in a world of innocence where priests and swashbucklers can coincide.

— Matthew Pinto

Michael Pinto and his swashbuckling brothers, Andrew and James, can be seen at www.AmazingGraceOnLine.net/Heart

PRAYER

*Jesus, thank you for your
presence in the Blessed
Sacrament and in our world.
Help me to take time to
recognize your presence
in all the events and things
of life. Help me to take time
to be quiet with you.*

*Jesus, keep me close to your
Sacred Heart.
Amen*

A HOLY HOUR FOR YOU

Dear _____

Today I offered an hour of prayer for the intentions closest to your heart.

With love and God's Blessings from

_____

Ascension Catholic Church
Adoration Chapel
Melbourne, FL

True Love

Looking into the face of my newborn baby girl, I was overcome with awe—at her helplessness, at her beauty, at her fragile innocence, at the fact that someone could have given her to us. You see, my wife Sharon and I had prayed for a baby for ten long years. As the months turned into years and the hole in our hearts felt bottomless, even imagining holding a baby of our own became difficult. Would there ever be a precious little soul for us to wrap in our love?

Jamie became pregnant at fifteen while dating the local "bad boy." He convinced her he would love her even more if she would just give in to him. Instead, Jamie learned his love was never there to begin with. Although the relationship ended, he pressured her to have an abortion. Her friends agreed with him.

As the months passed and Jamie's belly grew, she knew she could never end this life, but neither could she support a child. She was still a child herself, to be sure, but through her motherhood she matured beyond her years. Shopping and boys, makeup and music were the trivial pastimes of her youth. Now, she had a soul to nurture. Jamie loved the little heartbeat that thumped quietly next to hers. She loved it more than words could explain, more than she imagined she was capable of. But more than wanting her baby, Jamie wanted *for* her baby. She chose Sharon and me as a gift to her baby—two loving parents.

In the hospital, Jamie stood by her decision not to hold Hannah, fearing she might weaken and be unable to go through with the adoption. On the day Jamie went home, she wanted to see her baby. As I held her up through the nursery window, tears of both joy and agony washed down her cheeks. For the second time in as many days I was overcome with awe.

Hannah just had her first birthday. Every minute of the first year has been a reassurance to us of the goodness of our Creator. We recently asked Jamie if she would like to meet Hannah. "Only if you're sure it won't confuse or upset her," was Jamie's reply. "I just want her to be happy."

That teenage girl, who sought love in the wrong places, has taught me the real meaning of true love.

— Ken Kniepmann

Ken Kniepmann is a senior vice president for GreatEmployers.com, an Internet job board. Ken resides with his wife and two children in east-central Florida.

Chapter 3
He Picked Me Up When I Was Down

Angel Hair

The year was 1944. America was at war and everything was rationed or in very short supply, including Christmas trees. My father was four years old and, earlier that year, his mother had a very difficult pregnancy. The baby was born but did not survive. Three days later, on Good Friday, his mother died from complications associated with the delivery. It was a very difficult year for my dad, his father, and his five brothers and sisters.

My grandfather, John, worked for the post office and was, as usual, extremely busy as Christmas approached. He would work the midnight shift, come home, do his best to care for his six children, get some rest, and start over again, all while working through his own grief. In prior years, he always took off on Christmas Eve. The family would buy a Christmas tree and decorate it together in the afternoon. They would have dinner and then go to bed early so they could make it to the solemn 5:30 a.m. Mass to celebrate Christ's birth. Given the shortage of workers caused by the war, my grandfather John had to go to work on Christmas Eve morning.

Dad's older brothers, Jack and Franny, realized that they needed to go shopping if the family was going to have a tree. They scoured the town, but all of the lots were empty. There was not a tree to be found in all of

Philadelphia. Discouraged and sad, they returned home empty-handed. They put on a brave face so that their four-year-old brother would not realize what was going on. It was going to be hard enough to face Christmas without Mom, and the empty space in the tree stand was just another visible reminder of the void they all felt.

When my grandfather came home from work, Jack and Franny gave him the bad news about the tree. He told them not to worry, that he was going to Church for confession. "Confession?" they thought. "How in the world is that going to get us a tree?"

My grandfather walked the three blocks to St. Barnabas feeling very distraught. He had no idea how he was going to find a tree. He talked to his wife, Catherine, in heaven, and asked her to talk to God and find some way to help him.

The pastor, Father LaRue, heard his confession and at the end could tell something was still wrong. "Is there something else, John?" he asked. My grandfather told him he was without a tree for his children and he didn't know what to do. Well aware of John's loss of his wife, he was immediately overcome with a sense of "we can't let this happen."

Fr. LaRue left the confessional, telling John to follow him. He took him to the entrance of the church. "Take one of these," he said. Guarding the entrance to the church were two evergreens, standing like great sentinels fifteen-feet tall. Father LaRue helped John cut one and drag it to the sidewalk. He then returned to the confessional.

While their dad was at confession, the older children helped put the younger ones to bed, with their heads full of the normal Christmas expectations. Jack and Franny were sitting in the living room when their older sister, Mary, shouted from the front door, "Come quick! It's Dad and he's carrying something big!" They sprang up and ran out to meet him. The three of them then dragged the huge tree the rest of the way home. They had to cut it just to get it into the house. The giant tree filled the void in the stand and covered the living room in Christmas green!

The older children set about decorating the tree and after they had hung the last ornament, their Dad got out a special box of angel hair. Everyone remembered how Mom always put the angel hair on last, putting a clump on the tree to tell the younger children that Santa's beard must have gotten caught in the tree while he was leaving gifts.

That year, as my grandfather hung the angel hair, he could not help but think of his angel, his wife Catherine, in heaven, and the role she must have played in getting a tree for her family. That Christmas tree in 1944 told John, Mary, Jack, Franny and the others that even without Mom, things were going to be all right. It was clearly a message of hope.

Our family continues the tradition of hanging angel hair as the last tree decoration on Christmas Eve. As we place it, we remember Catherine and John and all of our family and friends in heaven—the angels we believe are praying for us.

— Matthew Manion

Matthew Manion's mission in life is to increase or restore people's faith in God, themselves, and others. As the President and CEO of the Catholic

Leadership Institute, he is committed to helping individuals fulfill their God-given potential as Catholic leaders and Christian witnesses in their family, workplace, community, and church. Matt has delivered leadership-training programs throughout the United States and has even had the privilege of carrying the Olympic Torch in 2002. He and his wife, Kerri, reside in Wayne, Pennsylvania, with their "amazing" daughter, Grace Anne.

A Carpenter and His Son

In the spring of 1989, I stood behind our house holding a hammer in one hand and a saw in the other. I realized I had bitten off more than my little five-foot, one-hundred-fifteen pound frame could handle. Great! I thought. Where is a carpenter when you need one? And then the tears started running down my cheeks.

For months we had been trying desperately to sell our house. My husband had fallen ill, and we needed to raise money to get him into an experimental cancer program in Tennessee. The program would cost $35,000, and it was not covered by insurance because it was not an approved medical procedure. We were having an open house the next weekend, but we discovered that the deck had rotted out.

I was one frustrated and tired lady. I had prayed for so many months and had tried so hard to be strong. This particular day I felt a bit cross with my beloved heavenly intercessors. "Saint Joseph," I said in the midst of my teary outburst, "you are not a very good real estate agent. Between praying to you and Father Solanus Casey (a Canadian priest who is up for canonization), I thought you two could handle a small problem like selling this house. Now what am I going to do? I need a professional carpenter and I cannot afford to hire one."

I had begun to sob in earnest when I heard a voice beside me say, "May I help you? I was just moving in next door and came around the side to get in the back of the garage. Looks like you have a problem."

I was very embarrassed to be caught crying and standing in the rubble of what once was a twenty-by-fifteen-foot foot deck. I had taken down the deck with a sledge hammer. I must have been an odd sight to this poor stranger who just happened to witness my latest disastrous situation. I wiped away my tears, told him of my problem and my foolish idea that I could rebuild the deck by myself. He looked up to the second story where the deck once stood fifteen-feet off the ground and then back at me with my ten-foot ladder, the only other tool I could find for the job. We both began to laugh.

My dear St. Joseph must not have been too insulted with my prayer. "Say," the man said, "my son and I can build that deck for you. We are pretty good carpenters." I agreed and he went next door, returning with his son and some very impressive professional power tools.

They set to work and by the next day, the deck was rebuilt. I had not bought enough lumber, but he managed to salvage some from the old deck to finish the job. As he and his son were picking up their tools, I thanked them profusely. They refused to take any money for their work.

Just before they left I happened to ask: "By the way, what do you do for a living? You should get into building decks. This is better than some professional carpenters I know could do." He grinned and handed me his business card: *Joseph's Decking Company, New and Existing Home Construction.*

— Christine Trollinger

Christine Trollinger is the author of several of the stories in this book. Her biography appears after The Badge of Grace *in Chapter One.*

Last Laugh

Walking out of my manager's office with my severance package under my arm, I knew this fellow parishioner was sincere when he told me it was one of the most difficult things he ever had to do. My lay-off was due to the fact that our company, like most of the telecommunications industry, had fallen on very difficult times.

Long before this day arrived, I had grown unhappy at work. A competitor had bought our company a few years before and the morale seemed to go downhill, right along with our stock price and our retirement plans. Still, after nearly eleven years of working for the same company and seeing jobs in the industry dry up, I was willing to hang on to pay the mortgage and provide for my family.

Just prior to this, I had begun praying for the intercession of St. Joseph the Worker to remain employed. My plan had been to wait until things picked up for our industry then seek employment elsewhere. I had forgotten what Mother Teresa used to say: "If you want to make God laugh, tell Him your plans."

As I began to clean out my desk that day, I thought of an old friend and past coworker, Dan. I gave him a call. Dan was stunned when I told him I was laid off. When he asked if I wanted another position like I once held with a manager who was difficult to work with, my first response was, "Oh, no."

Dan persisted, saying he thought I would really like the job working under Jack, with whom we both had worked with in the past. "But didn't Jack move to Paris?" I asked.

"He just moved back and you won't believe it—his office is right here in town," Dan said. "As a matter of fact, I had lunch with him last week. He told me he was going to hire someone for the job. I happened to know the candidate and told Jack the guy isn't qualified. You should call him."

I thanked Dan for the tip and told him that I was so fed up with telecommunications that I was considering trying another field, but that I would call Jack. I called him the next afternoon, but found he was on business in Paris, so I sent an e-mail. Jack answered me in less than two hours asking to get together the following Monday. As I researched the company Jack worked for, I continued to pray to St. Joseph the Worker.

Monday afternoon came around and I found myself in Jack's office, comparing stories about what we each had done since we first worked together. He described the type of role he was looking to have filled and I shared some of my ideas with him. After about half an hour of discussion, he looked at me and asked, "So when can you start?"

What an incredible blessing! Less than one week after being laid off, I was offered a job I knew would be just right for me. We agreed on a salary and I also made one final request before practically skipping out the door. "It took me ten years to get to the point where I earned four weeks of annual vacation. You don't suppose I could start with four weeks here do you?" He told me he would check.

My drive home was filled with prayers of thanksgiving to God and to St. Joseph the Worker. I prayed that by my work at this new company, God would be glorified and I would, through my work and through sharing my faith, be a worthy apostle for Him in this new job.

A few days later, I was told the company could not accommodate my request for four weeks of vacation this year. Instead, they would increase my salary. Only later did I learn that the company's policy would allow me five weeks vacation per year starting the following January.

Just a few months after I left my old company, some of the executives were found to have been involved in the most massive corporate fraud in United States history. The company went into bankruptcy.

Mother Teresa was right. God must have laughed when I told Him my plans because He had a better one than I ever would have imagined. Not only do I have a job I love, but I have been overseas four times since then. By His grace, I've been able to visit places I would never have dreamed of: Notre Dame, Sacre Coeur, Versailles, and the Church where Our Blessed Mother spoke to St. Catherine Laboure. God may have had the first laugh, but now I am joyfully laughing with Him.

— Cary Cusumano

Cary Cusumano is a graduate of the United States Naval Academy and a recent (May 1999) convert to the Catholic faith. He currently lives in Ashburn, Virginia with his wife and two children.

Ezekiel Bread

While I was away from the Catholic Church but still a very committed Christian, the conviction grew in me to preach. My wife, Emily, and I were living in Pella, Iowa, at the time. I had worked in Christian radio, and later managed a gas station as a means to meet people and talk to them about Jesus.

My desire ultimately was to become a pastor. So, with Emily's support, I enrolled in a ten-week pastor's training course in Bradenton, Florida. The school, the Institute of Ministry, was located on the Manatee River. It also served as a retreat center and family camp.

Life at school was good but not easy. Emily stayed behind in Iowa while I tried to survive on a meager budget. I rented a small room in an old man's trailer on the grounds of the retreat center, a trailer without air conditioning. During my first month, I ate very sparingly. There was a man at school who was a baker and made what was called "Ezekiel bread" from the ingredients given in the book of Ezekiel. For a dollar a loaf, this high-protien bread made from lentils, honey, and wheat, sustained me quite well. During my first month at school, I survived on one loaf a day. Emily sent me the little bit of money she could scrape together, but it was not much. I did not want her to worry, so I kept my daily menu to myself.

By the end of the month, I was famished (not to mention tired of the bread). Imagine my surprise when the guy who lived with me in the trailer asked if I would like some steak and eggs one morning.

"Yeah!" I exclaimed, my mouth watering.

"Great!" he replied. "That'll be five dollars for the steak." I waited for him to tell me he was just kidding. He did not. I thanked him for his offer and told him I was not so hungry after all.

After surviving a month solely on Ezekiel bread, I brought my hunger to the Lord. "Lord, I need help," I prayed. "I can't go for another two months just eating this bread."

One night shortly thereafter, I was sitting in the trailer studying when I heard a knock at the door. I opened it and there stood, not a flock of quail, but a young Hispanic student at the school. He held a bag of groceries in his arms.

"I was praying and the Lord told me that you needed food," he said. "My dad owns a grocery store, so ... here." He handed me the bag. In it there were more than ten steaks as well as pasta and many other foods. I could not believe it! In fact, I still get choked up thinking about it to this day. There was so much food that I wound up tithing it by giving some to others who were hungry as well. For the next month or so, I had enough to eat and more. Plus, he later brought over several more loads of food. I firmly believed in Christ's promise: "Ask and you shall receive," but to receive so much was overwhelming. I will never forget this tremendous grace!

— Jeff Cavins

Christmas Angels

Mentally going over my Christmas list in 1988, I reassured myself that I had not forgotten anyone. Still, an unshakable feeling that something was forgotten haunted me. Of course, I knew why that "missing" feeling hung on despite all the gift-wrapped packages tucked away. I just did not know what to do about it.

You see, our family had been struggling with the devastation of cancer for many months that year. My husband's cancer had returned with a vengeance and our three children had been diagnosed with the predisposition for this same hereditary cancer, one which had claimed my husband's mother at the age of thirty-three. The outlook was bleak to say the least. We were still trying to cope with the on-going battle as well as the loss of my sister-in-law that October; she also died at age thirty-three.

As Christmas approached, we tried to keep things normal for the children. Our family tradition had always been a joyous family affair. We would lavish decorations on our tree and the outside of the house and bake Christmas goodies. Then we would invite all the neighbors in for the lighting ceremony and to enjoy cookies, hot chocolate, and Christmas carols.

This year, there was no real celebration; we were merely going through the motions. Gene was too ill to help with the outside lights so I went to the basement alone to retrieve them. He sorted the lights from the couch where he now spent most of his time recouping from the latest surgery. Our kids were also not in the Christmas spirit as they scattered to their bedrooms, silently dealing with the pain in their own way.

Feeling no joy, I set up the nativity scene in the front yard. It was merely tradition, with no hope of a better tomorrow. When all the lights and decorations were finished and the tree adorned, we all came to look at it but then turned away with heavy hearts. It looked as though Christmas would not come to our house that year; maybe it would never come again. We pronounced it good enough and retired to our rooms for the night. Silence shrouded our house and sleep brought little relief or sweet dreams.

The following morning we awoke to an icy white-out. A blizzard had blown through our area over night and dumped nearly three feet of snow. A heavy white blanket covered all the outside decorations, leaving our little nativity scene buried below the ice-encrusted front yard. One by one we looked out to see that the storm had wiped out what little joy I had tried to create. The desolation of Christmas was now complete. Our weak attempts had proved futile against nature, both inside and outside our home.

We had no more energy for pretending. The nativity would stay buried. As we all moved toward our kitchen for a quiet breakfast, strange sounds drifted in from the other side of our living room picture window. The faintest jingle of laughter pierced the air. Each of us moved back toward the window, drawn like a magnet. We looked out onto the front yard and saw a wondrous sight. There on their knees in the snow were three little angels. As we watched the scene unfold, more angels came to join them. They all wore mittens and giggled while they used their hands to dig the manger out of the snow. These particular angels looked very familiar though.

A little five-year-old angel named Megan had brought a baby blanket in which to wrap the Christ child. As Megan wrapped and hugged the baby, neighbors had come and joined the children. They came to sing to the Christ Child, to share their laughter and, most of all, their joy. They brought cookies, hot chocolate, Christmas carols, and laughter. What they especially brought us was the Christmas tradition our own hearts could not muster. They awakened our hope in the Christ child and gave us strength to face the New Year.

This special memory of Christmas, when God's grace outshone darkness and despair, lives on in our hearts.

The following months and years were often difficult, but praise God, my dear husband and all our children are still alive and healthy. The cancer has been in remission now for thirteen years—a miracle according to doctors. My husband is, as far as we know, the longest survivor of this rare inherited cancer. Now, we consider each day a gift from the Christ child.

— Christine Trollinger

Christine Trollinger has contributed several wonderful stories to this book. You'll find her biography after The Badge of Grace *in Chapter One.*

Words to Live By

❧ Kind words are short and easy to speak, but their echoes are truly endless. – *Mother Teresa*

❧ The best exercise for strengthening the heart is reaching down and lifting people up. – *Ernest Blevins*

❧ The world says, "the more you take, the more you have." Christ says, "the more you give, the more you are." – *Frederick Buechner*

❧ When were the good and the brave ever in a majority? – *Henry Thoreau*

❧ Any fool can criticize, condemn, and complain, and most fools do. – *Benjamin Franklin*

❧ If you hear that someone is speaking ill of you, instead of trying to defend yourself you should say, "He obviously does not know me very well, since there are so many other faults he could have mentioned." – *Epictectus*

❧ Let me tell you the secret that has led me to my goal. My strength lies solely in my tenacity. – *Louis Pasteur*

❧ The Lord can do great things through those who don't care who gets the credit. – *Helen Pearson*

❧ Consider the postage stamp: Its usefulness consists in the ability to stick to one thing until it gets there.
— *Josh Billings*

❧ The difference between perseverance and obstinacy is that one often comes from a strong will, and the other from a strong won't. — *Henry Ward Beecher*

❧ Lack of will power has caused more failure than lack of intelligence or ability. — *Flower A. Newhouse*

❧ I have been driven many times to my knees by the overwhelming conviction that I had absolutely no other place to go. — *Abraham Lincoln*

❧ If you want the last word, apologize. — *Anonymous*

❧ The deeds you do today may be the only sermon some people will hear today. — *St. Francis of Assisi*

❧ If I did not believe in God, I should still want my doctor, my lawyer, and my banker to do so.
— *G. K. Chesterton*

❧ True holiness consists in doing God's will with a smile. — *Mother Teresa*

❧ If you believe what you like in the Gospel, and reject what you don't like, it is not the Gospel you believe, but yourself. — *St. Augustine of Hippo*

❧ A pessimist sees the difficulty in every opportunity; an optimist sees the opportunity in every difficulty.
— *Sir Winston Churchill*

❧ A single sunbeam is enough to drive away many shadows. – *St. Francis of Assisi*

❧ Every evening I turn my worries over to God. He's going to be up all night anyway. – *Anonymous*

❧ The world is full of givers and takers; the takers may eat better, but the givers sleep better. – *Anonymous*

❧ Once in the lobby of the Midland Hotel in Manchester when I happened to be in some public disfavor, a man came up to me, grasped my hand and observed: Never forget that only dead fish swim with the stream. – *Malcolm Muggeridge*

❧ The family that prays together stays together. (*Motto devised for the Roman Catholic Family Rosary Crusade, 1947, Al Scalpone*)

❧ The Holy Scriptures are our letters from home. – *St. Augustine of Hippo*

❧ We can do no great things, only small things with great love. – *Mother Teresa*

❧ All that we do without offering it to God is wasted. – *St. John Vianney*

From Grateful Dead to Gratefully Alive

"You'll never amount to anything," my high school principal snapped at me. I was in his office for getting into a fight with another student. Sure, I had supplied him with plenty of evidence that this would be the case, but his words stung nonetheless. Rather than fight his prediction, I soon confirmed it by dropping out of school.

An earring, waist-length hair, and years of self-destructive living provided strong evidence that my principal would be right. And had it not been for Our Lady, this might have been the case. But the Blessed Mother, like my own earthly mother, never gave up on me, thanks be to God!

The only external evidence of my journey on the road to perdition that remains is the Grateful Dead tattoo on my left shoulder. My "before and after" appearance is dramatic, but it is nothing compared to the internal changes wrought by God's grace.

During my early years I experienced many changes in family life. My mother was always a loving and caring woman, but my father drank a lot, eventually causing them to separate when I was about four years old.

When I was ten my mother remarried, and that same year she and my step-dad had me baptized into the Episcopal church. It is my first memory of anything even remotely related to God. Though I was newly baptized, religion did not become a part of my family life. I vaguely recall eating donuts after church, so I must have been to a service or two. I was so illiterate when it came to religion, I had no clue who St. Joseph, the angels and saints, or the Blessed Mother were. Even worse, I honestly thought Jesus was a mythical character who showed up at

Christmas along with Santa Claus. I knew nothing, not even a prayer.

My step-dad was in the Navy, so we relocated often. My parents had my little brother within the first year of their marriage and I started giving them trouble soon afterwards. By the time I was thirteen and we were living in Southern California, I was already involved with drugs and girls. It must have been a relief to my parents when my dad became stationed in Japan—a chance to get me away from bad influences. Instead, I became such a bad influence on my own that the country of Japan kicked me out ... once they were able to track me down.

It took a month for the military police to find me after I ran away from home. My parents were sick with worry. The naval authorities and Japanese officials were not so sympathetic, but equally as motivated to find me. It did not take much detective work to determine that the white boy regularly spotted at crime scenes was guilty. My dad's tour of duty ended nine months early. I was creating an international scene.

Before I was captured, my mom left with my little brother for my dad's next duty station in Pennsylvania, to prepare a home. But prior to leaving, at the offer of a Filipino friend, both my mom and dad started attending Catholic services. My parents were desperate for help with their out-of-control son, and the Catholic Church offered them great consolation and hope. It was not long before they joined the Church. Although my mom returned to the States heart-broken without me, she now had a source of comfort and strength—God.

The military police brought me to jail in handcuffs. Two days later I was released to my stepfather, but military police were in attendance, lest I try to run away again.

Not until I stepped off the plane in the United States were the handcuffs removed. My step-dad treated me with great love and kindness, but I wanted none of it. When I saw my mom again, she cried tears of joy and hugged me, but I brushed her off. I hated my parents for taking me out of my paradise.

Part of the agreement the Navy made with the Japanese authorities not to press charges required me to enter a rehabilitation center. I managed to run away once, but was easily caught and ended up completing the ten-week program. I think everyone knew I did not take the program seriously.

The wall I built between my parents and me was impenetrable and nothing, especially religion, was going to get through. I had no desire to give up my drugs and womanizing.

It was around this time I quit school. I hit rock bottom in life. A girl I really cared for broke up with me, and I soon realized I was not capable of maintaining a relationship. I felt like a total loser. I was desperate. I could not stand being me anymore. I went to rehab for a second time in Philadelphia. Although their intention was to challenge me by telling me the odds were against my ever succeeding, instead I felt: "Why bother, I'm hopeless."

When I turned eighteen, I bummed around the East Coast for a while with a friend. My travels included heavy partying and another night in jail on a misdemeanor before returning home. My life was going nowhere, and I was miserable.

One evening, while planning for a night out with friends, a terrible feeling came over me. Something was coming for me and I could only imagine that it was death.

I canceled my plans. The feeling lingered. I realized it did not matter what I did that evening, I was going to confront something. Whatever it was, I wanted to be home when it happened.

Sitting in my room, I became restless. I wanted to go out but did not dare. Fighting boredom, I walked into the hall and scanned my parent's bookshelf. Shakespeare, poetry...nothing interesting...then one book caught my eye. I pulled it out and scanned it. It was a book on apparitions of the Blessed Mother.

I flipped through and saw pictures of children looking up at a vision of a lady. Stupefied, I read the captions. "My parents are into some kind of a cult!" I thought with horror.

Fascinated, I took it to my room and began reading. At 3 a.m. I closed the book, having read it from cover to cover. I had no idea who the Blessed Mother was, but when I started to read about things like prayer, fasting, Jesus Christ, and His death on the Cross for me, I was overcome with a sense of love and joy. Much of it I did not even understand. When I put the book down I said to myself, "This woman is the woman I have always been looking for. This Virgin Mary is perfect. Her God is my God. I will listen to whatever she tells me."

My euphoric excitement made sleep impossible. I could not wait until my mom woke up so I could share my enthusiasm with her. My whole life had been flipped upside down. When my mom did finally wake up, I shakily told her I wanted to talk to a Catholic priest. Stunned, she asked me to repeat what her ears could not believe. I showed her the book I had read.

"You read that book?" Mom asked incredulously.

"Mom, I consumed the book," I exclaimed.

"Whoever Mary is, whoever Jesus is, and that bread...I know it's all true. I want to talk to a priest!"

There was a Catholic chaplain on base. I literally ran the half-mile to see him at Our Lady of Victory chapel. He did not know what to make of me—long hair, earring, funky clothes—radically out of place for a military base.

"Who are you and where did you come from?" he wanted to know.

I tried to tell him everything in a few sentences. Not knowing what to make of me and having another appointment, he gave me a crucifix, a picture of the Sacred Heart of Jesus and one of Pope John Paul II, and told me to return the next day. I skipped home with my treasures. Then, I got five big garbage bags and filled them with clothes, music, drug paraphernalia—anything I was attached to. My mom stood back silently in amazement and left me alone.

I hung the crucifix and pictures around my room. Then, I did not know what to do while I waited to see the priest the next day so I looked through the book again. A desire welled up in me to talk to God and Our Lady so I knelt in front of the Sacred Heart picture and waited. I thought, "Well, okay, I'm ready." I had no idea what prayer was all about and expected God to appear to me.

As I looked upon the image of Jesus, however, I became flooded with real contrition and joy. Tears poured down from my eyes for at least an hour, leaving my clothes soaked. I was completely convicted of my sinfulness and of God's love. I knew there was hope for me. I knew I would never be the same. The old me had died the night before.

The next day the priest was again busy and asked me to go to the back of the church where he would say Mass and then we could talk afterwards. I did so, but when

Father came in wearing a white robe (his vestments), and everyone stood at the same time, I was confused. "Is this some sort of choreographed play?" I wondered.

I watched curiously as everyone kneeled while Father raised a white circle. At that moment, the depths of my being cried out, "There is my God!" I was infused with the knowledge that it was Jesus Christ. I knew it, I knew it, and I wanted to receive Him so badly.

After Mass I confronted the priest: "When you raised the white circle, that was God, wasn't it! I know it, that was God! Tell me that was God!"

I wondered why I never knew about all this before. It was what I always wanted. It was the meaning in life that would be everlasting. And the perfect woman I had been searching for, I found in Mary. Everything fell into place.

I overwhelmed quite a few people in the months ahead. My stepdad was one of them. He had been away at sea on an aircraft carrier and happily returned to a completely changed son. Six months later, when I was confirmed, his fatherly words meant the world to me. "Welcome home," he said. I had gone from hating my parents to realizing they were my best friends. And my little brother whom I had mostly ignored, became third in my life after God and Mary.

In 1993, after only ten months as a Catholic, I said good-bye to the happiest mom in the world, on my way to be a priest with the Congregation of Marians of the Immaculate Conception. This radical life of poverty, chastity and obedience—the very things I once ran from—I now embrace.

My calling to the priesthood is like a marriage covenant with God. The honeymoon—the high of my conversion—lasted four years. It was as if God gave me a lollipop experience so I could taste the sweetness of His love. Then He took the lollipop away so I had to struggle and still choose Him. That is where the real love is; to remain faithful when it is not always easy. Our Lady is the one who brought me to Jesus and I continue to go to Him through her. I've been saved by Jesus with the cooperation of His Blessed Mother.

— Fr. Donald Calloway

Fr. Donald Calloway was ordained a priest with the Congregation of Marians of the Immaculate Conception in May 2003. He went from a high school dropout to earning a bachelor's degree with a double major in philosophy and theology from the Franciscan University of Steubenville, and M.Div. and S.T.B. degrees from the Dominican House of Studies in Washington, DC. He is pursuing an S.T.L. degree from the International Marian Research Institute in Dayton, Ohio, and plans to continue studies for a Doctorate in Mariology.

See pictures related to this story at www.AmazingGraceOnLine.net/Heart

The Beatitudes

Blessed are the poor in spirit,
for theirs is the kingdom of heaven.

Blessed are those who mourn,
for they shall be comforted.

Blessed are the meek,
for they shall inherit the earth.

Blessed are those who hunger and thirst for righteousness,
for they shall be satisfied.

Blessed are the merciful,
for they shall obtain mercy.

Blessed are the pure in heart,
for they shall see God.

Blessed are the peacemakers,
for they shall be called sons of God.

Blessed are those who are persecuted
for righteousness' sake,
for theirs is the kingdom of heaven.

Blessed are you when men revile you and persecute you
and utter all kinds of evil against you falsely on my
account. Rejoice and be glad, for your reward is great
in heaven.

— *Matthew 5:3-11*

Christmas Lullaby

"Ready or not here I come," my brother, Sparky, called as he played hide-and-seek with me and our Aunt Flo. Opening the closet door to discover Flo he shouted, "I found you. I found you!"

We all collapsed in a giggling heap on the floor. Finally Aunt Flo got up. We looked at her and realized it was time for the fun to end.

"Do we have to go back to Mrs. Muran's house?" Sparky tearfully asked. "Why can't we just stay here?"

It was the early 1940's and our daddy was away in the Army fighting someone called Hitler. Our mother was sick, we were told, and unable to take care of us. At four years old, all I knew was that I wanted my mommy and daddy. We had been placed in an unloving foster home but were allowed to visit Grandma, Grandpa, and our teenage Aunt Flo on most weekends.

As Aunt Flo helped us with our coats, I cried quietly and Sparky reached out and patted my shoulder. Grammy came in and pulled us close. "We'll all be together soon. You'll see."

Flo put her arms around us and sang softly, "Tura, lura lura, tura lura li, tura lura lura hush now don't you cry..." Our grandfather joined in singing the Irish lullaby with his sweet tenor voice. Then he helped us put on our new mittens. "Be brave now," he said. "We'll see you again at Christmas."

I began sobbing. Flo took us by the hand, to begin the long walk to the bus that would take us back to Mrs. Muran's house, the foster home.

Mr. and Mrs. Muran were mean and short-tempered with us and the other foster kids placed there. Mrs. Muran hit us with a strap when she got mad and Mr. Muran used his cane. I once overheard Flo tell Grammy: "Mother, it is just like a prison. Even animals are treated better than that."

"Yes, I know." Grandma had said in a hushed voice. "We are doing everything we can, Florence, but the law says their mother can place them anywhere she pleases. That doesn't mean we are going to give up trying to have them live with us though."

We loved to visit our grandparents, but most of all we loved being with Aunt Flo. She would help us get ready for bed, read stories and nursery rhymes, and teach us about Jesus. One night Aunt Flo told us that Jesus loved us, and that He gave us each an angel to watch over us. I called my angel a "Garden Angel.

"Garden Angels don't come to Mrs. Muran's house." I told her one night.

"Oh yes they do. Your angel goes everywhere you go."

"But not to Mrs. Muran's house," Sparky piped up, "Because she doesn't like angels. She said so. Some people said you were an angel and then she got mad. She said, 'We don't need no angels like her around here.'"

"Mrs. Muran says Santa doesn't come to her house either," I told Flo, "but that's OK because baby Jesus still comes on Christmas," I told Aunt Flo.

As we walked to the bus stop, Aunt Flo talked about our Christmas plans. We would go to Mass at St. John's Church and see the pretty red flowers and candles around the altar and hear the choir sing "Away In A Manger" and "Silent Night." Then she would help us get ready for bed

in our new pajamas, tell us the story of the first Christmas
and sing Christmas carols and also our favorite Irish lullaby. Christmas morning we would see the Christmas tree
all decorated and maybe Santa would even leave presents
for us.

When Christmas Eve day came, all the other kids at
Mrs. Muran's left one by one. It was snowing hard and we
stared out the window waiting for Flo. Then we saw her
go around to the back door. We were so excited, but Mrs.
Muran chased us up the stairs and told us to go to the attic.
That's where we slept. We went only part of the way up
and stopped to listen.

Flo knocked on the back door. She knocked and knocked,
louder and louder. Finally Mrs. Muran jerked the door
open, "What do ya want?" she yelled. "Oh it's you."

"I came to pick up the kids."

"Those brats ain't goin nowhere. Mostly not with the
likes of you. All's ya do is spoil 'em rotten." Mrs. Muran
raged.

"What do you mean? It's Christmas and their mother
said we could take them," Flo said in a strained voice.

"Well she ain't told me nothin' 'bout them goin with
ya, so get out of here."

"Flo, Flo," we called, running to the door behind Mrs.
Muran, "take us home with you, please."

Flo tried again. "Mrs. Muran, it is Christmas Eve and
I figure you and your husband could use some time without children around, so..."

"Well ya figure wrong," she interrupted. "Now get
outta here or I'll call the cops, ya hear!"

"Well, you can at least give them this one present," Flo
said, her voice increasing in volume. Mrs. Muran tore the
wrapping paper from the package Flo handed her.

"Pajamas! what they need these things for?" she screamed loudly. "They'll not be needen those around here. Their underwear is good enough, just like all the others. We don't do no spoilin,' ya hear? We don't have no Christmas either."

We were crying but didn't want to make Flo feel bad. "It's okay Flo, cause Baby Jesus will bring His angel." I called to her. "You'll see."

"I love you," Flo called, then yelled at Mrs. Muran. "You mean witch. How could you do this? It's Christmas." Flo was crying. I never saw her cry like that before.

Mrs. Muran threw the pajamas at Flo and slammed the door shut.

"Don't worry," Flo called to us. "I'll come back to get you."

Mrs. Muran yelled at us, "Get up the stairs and inta bed, the two of ya and fast." The attic was cold and dark that night. It was lonely without the other kids. We laid down, shivering on the big old bed. It didn't have any sheets or covers. Mrs. Muran opened the door and threw in an old blanket. "Put this on and get to sleep, ya hear me?"

"Yes ma'am," we said. We were glad to have the blanket. It helped some, and Sparky pulled me closer to help me get warm.

"Jesus will come with His angel," I said. "You'll see."

"Shh, go to sleep."

I went to sleep for awhile, but soon awakened. It was dark and cold in the room, but light was shining in the window. I got out of bed and went over to the window and looked below. I could hear someone singing. It was soft, but I could hear her.

"What are you doing?" Sparky whispered

"Shh, can't you hear her?"

Sparky listened with his ear up to the window. "Hear who?"

"The angel! She's singing the Christmas lullaby for us. Jesus did it. He brought His angel! I told you he would!"

Once again Sparky listened, and slowly a sweet voice rose singing: "Tura lura, lura, tura lura li, tura lura lura, hush now don't you cry. Tura lura lura, tura lura li, tura lura lura, that's a Christmas lullaby."

We knew Flo's voice. Suddenly a second voice softly sang "Away in a Manger" as Flo sang the Christmas Lullaby. We peeked out and saw Aunt Flo smiling up at us, but no one else was there!. The light from the moon was shining on the snow and a bright star was in the sky. Flo waved at us.

We felt warm even though the room was cold. We knew the tiny Baby of Bethlehem was with us, sharing His love. We fell asleep listening to the singing, lying there by the window, with the old blanket wrapped around us.

The next morning, Flo came to take us with her. To our surprise Mrs. Muran offered no protest. She had even packed up all our clothes. "Get them outta here fast now, ya hear me? And don't be coming around here again, none of ya. I'll not be having you with your magic and ghosts and such. Now get!"

"Yes Mrs. Muran," Flo said and grabbed our bag. Flo winked at us, and held a finger up to her lips so we wouldn't talk. Then she took our hands and we all ran down the driveway, to the walk, and up the corner to catch the bus.

We didn't know what Mrs. Muran had seen, but we knew what we had seen and it wasn't a ghost.

"Baby Jesus came last night, Flo," I told her. "He brought two angels."

"No He didn't," Sparky said emphatically, "That was Flo singing, silly.'

"Who were the two angels?" Flo wanted to know.

"Well, one was my Garden Angel," I said. "She sang 'Away in A Manger.'"

"So that's what she meant." Flo said, her eyes wide. "Who was the other angel?"

"Jesus didn't need another Garden Angel 'cause he had you. And you sang the Christmas lullaby."

We did all the things Flo told us we would do on Christmas, but the best gift was our new home with our grandparents. We were raised by our grandparents, and to this day, fifty years later, Flo is more than our aunt— she is an angel to us.

— Ann Catherine Howerton

Ann Catherine Howerton, wife, mother of three grown children, and grandmother of three beautiful grandchildren, is a retired home health nurse. She loves to write of the people God has sent into her life. Ann Catherine is currently working on another book in the Amazing Grace series titled Amazing Grace for Those Who Heal. *She lives with her husband in Eugene, Oregon.*

See pictures related to this story at www.AmazingGraceOnLine.net/Heart

Picking up the Pieces

Twenty years ago I sat by my phone living the nightmare every military wife fears: waiting to hear if my husband, Mike, was dead or alive. Mike was a major in the United States Air Force. After a wonderful, relaxing morning together on May 12, 1982, in our North Little Rock, Arkansas, home, he had left to take some pilots up in a C-130 for a check-ride.

I had put our four young boys to bed at their usual 8 p.m. bedtime. A friend called about 8:30 and came over because she had heard there was an accident and she feared Mike could be involved. I called the squadron to speak to Mike. "He's not here right now," I was told. I called again at 9:30 and 10:30. Still, Mike was not there. Two other friends came over during this time. We sat, prayed and awaited word.

"Please God," I prayed, "take his arms or his legs or whatever You want, but give him his life; we need him."

At midnight, I watched the local news. The Air Force reported that there had been a serious accident of a C-130. An undetectable crack in the wing spread during flight and cracked off, causing the engine to explode. The plane was flying at fifteen hundred feet. All seven aboard died. I called the squadron again, "I know it's Mike," I cried. "I know he died. Please do not send the blue Air Force car." Instead, I asked them to send Mike Scott, one of my husband's friends.

Trembling and weak, I went to the door when I heard Scott's car pull up. "It's Mike isn't it?" I whispered.

"Yes," he said quietly. Hearing the words hit me like a sledge hammer. I collapsed. Scott had brought a priest and nurse with him. I sat in the living room for hours with everyone; numb, crying, drained of even my thoughts. By morning, one friend remained. Another priest came about 6 a.m. to help me tell my sons.

Around 6:30, the children began to waken. Taking a deep breath, I went into eleven-year-old Jeff's room. He looked out the window at the cars and then at me. "Mom," he said, "Daddy died, didn't he?"

I cried and hugged him and explained that the plane his dad was flying had crashed. One by one I told the others: Greg, nine, Charles, six, and Tim, four. What followed afterwards is a blur. We returned to Mike's and my home state of North Dakota for the funeral. I chose to buy a house there and plan for the future as a single mother. But first, leaving the boys with their grandparents, I returned to Arkansas to sell our house and tie up loose ends.

That is when I fell apart. For days no one could get me to budge from the house. This had been where Mike and I had been happy. I could not leave it. Friends called a priest who came over at 10 a.m. and stayed with me until evening. The numbness had changed into anger. I cried and screamed. "Why did God have to take Mike?" It wasn't fair. Mike and I had been good Catholics. Not only did we go to church every Sunday, but we volunteered and provided a good Catholic upbringing for our boys. I even frequently went to daily Mass. "We did everything God wanted us to do," I cried. "Why is He doing this to us?"

Father listened and prayed with me. He offered no answers except to repeatedly tell me, "You are going to be okay." By evening I was ready to leave the house with a friend. In the morning, I went to Mass and prayed the Rosary. I prayed for strength and direction. Without Mike, I had neither. One thing I did know was that Mike wanted me to take care of our children and raise them Catholic.

I returned to North Dakota to put our lives together. We settled into a routine, but my heart was not in it. I had no desire to return to daily Mass. Sundays were enough. God had taken away what I loved, why should I do more than the minimum? Still, I prayed and kept asking God for direction and for the emptiness to go away. I felt so alone. The nearest relative was two hundred miles away. My biggest concern was for my boys. A mother could only do so much. I could not take Mike's place.

Soon after we moved in, people started showing up in our lives, from the neighborhood and from church. I returned to daily Mass. I still was not happy with God, but where else could I go? I could not understand His ways, but I knew I needed Him. It took almost two years for me to feel that I was healing. One day I noticed thick dust on the television in the basement. It hit me that I was acting as a custodian to my kids, as if, without Mike, I could not give completely. With that realization, I put away my wedding ring and bought a mother's ring with four stones. I could not take the place of a father, but I could fully commit myself to my boys.

I became totally involved in their activities. Every night I went from bed to bed, individually praying and talking with each boy as I held his hand. I recruited the husbands of friends and other willing men to serve as role models and help take Mike's place. With four boys and four sets of activities, anytime two activities coincided, I often sent one of the boys to be there for his brother. We even went on family vacations. Mike's void was never completely gone, but it was filled in with Boy Scout leaders, coaches, teachers, family and friends—and God. I never stopped missing Mike, but he was a part of our lives. I could often feel his arms around us. I frequently reminded the boys: "Remember, God sees you and so does Dad."

One Sunday after Mass, we went to the education center for doughnuts. Tim overheard someone tell me that the boys were turning out well. When we got into the car, eight-year-old Tim took his hand and turned my face towards him. "It's not because of you that we are doing good," he informed me. "It's because we chose to do good." I chuckled and retold the story often. Years later Tim came to me and said, "Mom, the next time you tell that story, don't forget to add that you taught us how to choose."

I did not choose to lose Mike, but I did choose to turn back to God and trust Him once again. It was God's grace that kept us going without our husband and father. I thank Him for my wonderful boys and for the giving people He placed in our lives.

— Marsha Riely

Jeff, 32, is married and the father of one child. He graduated from University of North Dakota and is a pilot for Delta Airlines.

Greg, 30, is married and a graduate of Johns Hopkins University (B.S.) and Case Western Reserve University (M.D. and Ph.D.), and is currently doing his residency at New York Hospital.

Charles, 27, is married and the father of one child. He is a graduate of Yale University and the University of Michigan Law School. He works for Aikin Gump Law Firm, New York City.

Tim, 25, is a graduate of the University of Notre Dame. He is a technology consultant for Deloitte Consulting, Chicago.

Marsha stayed home full-time until the boys grew older. She went back to school to obtain her master's degree in nursing education, and she currently is an associate professor at Medcenter One College of Nursing. She is founder of Medcenter One's Good Grief bereavement program, has been named "nurse of the year" in North Dakota's District Six, and "faculty of the year" at Medcenter's College of Nursing.

See pictures related to this story at www.AmazingGraceOnLine.net/Heart

Always Believe

Upon exiting the operating room, Dr. John Witt of St. Alexius Hospital in Bismarck, North Dakota, approached his patient's husband and parents with some difficult news. "I'm sorry but Lois may not make it through the night," he said. "I've completed only half of the surgery I intended to do." Severe bleeding had caused a dangerous drop in Lois Mautz's blood pressure, thus precluding the removal of her uterus.

Recurring fibroids, called Asherman Syndrome, wove in and out of the uterus so that it had become inhospitable to life—the life of the child that Lois and her husband, Carey, so much desired since their marriage four years earlier.

Carey and Lois Mautz were married November 3, 1990 and wanted to start a family right away. She was twenty-eight and anxious to become a mother. "I had great parents," she says, "and I wanted to be like them." Her parents had taught her that God was always in control, that trust in Him would sustain her through any of life's trials. Little did Lois imagine that her faith would be tested to such a degree!

The couple was thrilled when their first baby was conceived in April, 1991. Their delight was short-lived, however. In August, the baby miscarried, apparently suffocated by inter-uterine fibroids. Lois needed surgery to remove the invading tissues. "It all seemed like a nightmare," she said, though it became her reality for several more years.

In December of the same year, Lois and Carey were expecting for the second time, and once again their joy knew no bounds. Though she found herself vacillating between elation and fear, Lois knew that in God's Providence, all would turn out the way it should. Just two months later, in February of 1992, heartache returned when this baby also died.

"I don't think God listens to my prayers," Carey told his wife with deep sadness. Lois assured him with affirmations such as, "Keep trusting, everything happens for a reason, and God's will be done." When two ob-gyn specialists informed the Mautzes that they would likely never have children, Lois had to lean heavily on her own words.

In April of 1994, four large fibroids which threatened to destroy any possibility of a child for the hopeful couple were scheduled for surgical removal. Dr. Witt warned the Mautzes that he would probably remove the uterus if he saw that it was too badly scarred from the recurring fibroids. Indeed, it was scarred, but after Lois' left ovary was removed, serious complications developed, halting the removal of the uterus. Dr. Witt had to abandon his plan to extract the only means for supporting the life of the baby they prayed for.

Because of her doctor's expert care, Lois survived the crisis. Returning to the conscious world, she asked almost immediately, "Do I still have my uterus?" When told that it had not been removed, she says, "that was music to my ears." She decided right then that she would accept the fact that she may never have a child. Once again, her faith played a strong role in her resolve to accept the hand dealt her. After all, she was alive and she and Carey were blessed with six godchildren who would be a part of their lives.

Lois and Carey did their best to surrender to God their hopes and dreams for a child, trying hard not to dwell on the subject too much. She continued her job as a hospital lab technician. Life seemed to just be getting back on an even keel when in October of 1995, a home pregnancy test revealed that Lois had conceived once more. Again the Mautzes were excited, even though they had already experienced such severe disappointments.

Dr. Witt, however, was not at all excited when Lois came in for her prenatal exam. He did not believe she could ever carry a child to term. "You are no longer my patient, but God's!" Dr. Witt declared. He ordered an ultrasound to determine the condition of the uterus. He was, however, not expecting what he saw: No scars and no adhesions! Lois's uterus looked totally normal. The word "miracle" passed over her doctor's lips.

The pregnancy advanced normally until January of 1996, when serious bleeding began. Lois was put on bed rest. The bleeding subsided in March, but as a precaution, bed rest was continued. Carey bargained with God that if their child survived, he would be a more faithful Catholic. Lois, for her part, had already decided on the baby's name, so sure was she that the Lord had spared her uterus in order for this child to be born.

It was two o'clock in the morning of June 17, 1996. The Mautzes, followed closely by Lois's anxious parents, raced to the hospital.

"It was a wild ride," Lois recalls. "I kept praying that we wouldn't hit a deer." An emergency surgery team assembled quickly, headed by Dr. Witt. Lois and Carey prayed and thanked God for the incredible miracle about to happen. At 6:08 a.m., Kendal Thomas Mautz was born, weighing a healthy 9 lbs., 1oz.

Tears of joy streamed down Carey's face as he gently placed little Kendal into his loving mother's arms. Six years of painful, emotional agony paled as Lois and Carey beheld their precious son. As she held her baby for the first time, a flood-gate of emotion swept over Lois—an incredible release of long years of tension and frustration.

As Lois says so eloquently, "It is truly God that carries our future in His hands." Carey agrees! Always believe!

— Nellie Edwards

Nellie Edwards' biography appears after A Valentine for Jesus (Almost) *in Chapter Two.*

The Rosebud

It is only a tiny rosebud, a flower of His design
But I cannot unfold the petals
with these clumsy hands of mine.
The secret of unfolding flowers
is not known to such as I;
The rose God opens so sweetly
in my hands would fade and die.
If I cannot unfold the rosebud,
the flower of His design
What makes me think I have wisdom
to unfold this life of mine?
So I'll trust him for his leading
each moment of every day
And I'll look to him for courage
each step of the pilgrim way.
For the path that lies before me,
my heavenly Father knows;
I'll trust him to unfold the moments
just as He unfolds the rose.

— Anonymous

Our Source of Grace

Jesus of Nazareth, without money or arms, conquered more millions than Alexander, Caesar, and Napoleon; without science and learning, He shed more light on things human and divine than all the philosophers and schools combined; without the eloquence of learning, He spoke words of life such as never were spoken before or since, and produced effects which lie beyond the reach of any orator or poet; without writing a single line, He has set more pens in motion, and furnished themes for more sermons, orations, discussions, learned volumes, works of art, and sweet songs of praise, than the whole army of great men of ancient and modern times.

Born in a manger and crucified as a criminal, He now controls the destiny of the world, and rules a spiritual empire which embraces one-quarter of the world's inhabitants. There was never in this world a life so unpretentious, modest, and lowly in its outward form and condition, and yet producing such extraordinary effects upon all ages, nations, and classes of men. The annals of history produce no other example of such complete and astonishing success in spite of the absence of those material, social, literary, and artistic powers and influences which are indispensable to success for a mere man.

His grace will sustain you in times of trial.

— An adaptation of a poem written by Phillip Schaff, an American theologian and historian of the 19th century.

Chapter 4

The Lighter Side of Grace

Let Me Out of Here!

My friend Celia Sattler often takes advantage of the confession offered prior to daily Mass. On one occasion, when it was her turn, Father Thomas Richter, a newly ordained priest, apologized and said he had run out of time to hear her confession but would be glad to do so after Mass. After Mass, Celia waited in the pews until she saw the green light over the confessional door, signaling that Fr. Tom had returned. It was a Friday, the usual day for church cleaning, so during confession the sounds of a vacuum cleaner reverberated through the door.

After her confession, Celia thanked Father and went to leave but found the door locked. Trying again in vain, she announced she could not get out. Apparently the janitor had locked the door, not realizing they were inside. Because of all the noise from the vacuum, neither Celia nor Fr. Tom had heard it lock.

"Well, turn the handle," Fr. Tom said.

"I am trying to," Celia answered. "It won't turn."

Fr. Tom came over from the other side of the screen to try the door himself. After he failed to pry it to open, Celia saw a look of panic cross his face. He placed his hands and forehead against the door and prayed aloud, "Dear God, please help us!!"

Fortunately, after a few shouts and loud banging on the door from Fr. Tom, a janitor soon came with the key.

With a grin he asked, "What's the matter Father? Did you get locked in with this lady?" Celia quickly slipped away, but she always thought she detected a sly grin from Fr. Tom thereafter.

She had never told this story before, and thought it might be good for this book. "Oh, I have one for you," she reported. Before using it, though, she wanted me to check with Fr. Tom and make sure he didn't mind.

Fr. Tom laughed loudly when he recalled the incident and said, "That was Celia?" Celia had made her confession behind a screen, but had assumed he knew her identity once he came over on her side. In actuality, Fr. Tom had still managed to maintain her privacy, despite the awkward situation. He backed out of his chair and looked down at his shoes while he yelled for help and pounded on the door. Fr. Tom initially told her to bang on the door and call for help herself so as not to intrude on her anonymity.

But then suddenly, he shot out of his chair in a panic and yelled, "No wait! I'll do it!" Being his first day on the job, it occurred to him that it would not make a good first impression in his new parish to have a lady's voice screaming from within his confessional: "Help someone! Let me out!"

Fr. Tom said he much preferred being greeted by the janitor's grin and comments than inciting the imaginations of the people still in church.

— Patti Maguire Armstrong

The Priest and the Politician

A parish priest was being honored at a dinner on the twenty-fifth anniversary of his arrival in that parish. A leading local politician, who was a member of the congregation, was chosen to make the presentation and give a little speech at the dinner, but he was delayed in traffic. So the priest decided to say a few words while they waited. "You understand," he said, "the seal of the confessional can never be broken. I can say, however, that I got my first impressions of the parish from the first confession I heard here over twenty-five years ago. I thought I had been assigned to a terrible place. The very first chap who entered my confessional told me how he had stolen a television set and, when stopped by the police, how he had almost murdered the officer. Furthermore, he told me he had embezzled money from his place of business and had an affair with his boss' wife. I was appalled. But as the days went by I discovered that not all my parishoners were like that, and that I had indeed come to a fine parish full of devout and loving people."

Just as the priest finished his talk, the politician arrived full of apologies at being late. He immediately began his presentation. "I'll never forget the first day Father arrived in this parish," said the politician. "In fact, I had the honor of being the first one to go to him in confession!"

Out of the Mouths of Babes

When I was about nine years old, I remember waiting in line with my parents to make our confession. My younger brother, Scott, seven years old, was in the confessional. This was in the 1960's and there were quite a few people of all ages lined up and waiting their turn.

Scott was unusually loud, which made it next to impossible not to hear him as he confessed. "Bless me Father for I have sinned," he shouted. The hushed murmurs of the priest were barely audible, but Scott's voice seemed to reverberate through the church.

"Well, I lied one time," he practically yelled. I looked at my parents, who exchanged glances and smirks with the other adults in line. Everyone kept a respectful distance from the confessional, but Scott could be heard through the church.

It was quiet for a moment, at which time the priest must have said a few words. Then, again, Scott's booming voice could be heard, this time even louder. "Well, I didn't want to lie," he shouted. "My mother made me do it!"

Now my mother's face quickly changed into a look of horror. Scott came out absolved of this "sin" inflicted on him and mom was next in line to talk to the priest, perhaps to do some explaining about the previous confession.

— Mark Armstrong

Mark Armstrong has been married to Patti, the co-editor of this book, for twenty-two years. Mark is the public relations manager for Workforce Safety & Insurance, North Dakota's workers' compensation organization.

Friar Untucked

"It's right here: DRY CLEAN ONLY."

Meatless Fridays

John Smith was the only Protestant to move into a large Catholic neighborhood. On the first Friday of Lent, John was outside grilling a big juicy steak. Meanwhile, all of his neighbors were eating cold tuna fish for supper. This went on each Friday of Lent. On the last Friday of Lent, the neighborhood men got together and decided that something had to be done about John. He was tempting them to eat meat each Lenten Friday, and they could not take it anymore. They decided to try and convert John to the Catholic faith. They went over and talked to him. After some persuasion, John decided to join his neighbors and become a Catholic, which made them all very happy. They took him to church, and the priest sprinkled some water over him, blessed him, and said, "You were born a Baptist, you were raised a Baptist, but now you are a Catholic." The men were so relieved, now that their biggest Lenten temptation was removed.

The next year's Lenten season rolled around. The first Friday of Lent came, and, just at supper time, when the neighborhood was settling down to their cold tuna fish dinner, the smell of steak cooking on a grill came wafting into their homes. The neighborhood men could not believe their noses. What was going on?

They called each other and decided to meet over in John's yard to see if he had forgotten it was the first Friday of Lent. The group arrived in time to see John standing over his grill with a small pitcher of water. He was sprinkling some water over his steak on the grill, saying, "You were born a cow, you were raised a cow, but now you are fish."

Monster in the Manger

I have to admit it. I pride myself somewhat on my son Michael's knowledge of the Bible. All those Bible story videos seem to be working. At just five-and-a-half years old, he already knows many of the people, places, and events of both the Old and New Testament.

Most nights before bed I read a story or two from a children's Bible my wife and I bought for our three young sons. Occasionally, I will stop the story in mid-sentence and pose a question to one of the boys to casually test their biblical literacy. One of Michael's recent answers took me by surprise.

We were reading about the birth of Jesus when I asked him about the three wise men. Feeling smug that he knew the obscure names of Melchoir, Caspar, and Balthasar, I posed another question—an easy one.

"What gifts did the three wise men bring to Jesus?"

Michael delayed for a second and then confidently said, "Gold, Frankenstein, and Myrrh."

Well, I guess it's back to the laboratory for those boys.

— Matthew Pinto

Cranial Cobwebs

A friend of mine used to get together with a group of women each week to share a devotional reading and spend time in prayer. One time, a particular lady in the group prayed, "Dear Lord, please remove the cobwebs from my mind, so that I can more clearly contemplate your love." The next week, her prayer was exactly the same: "Dear Lord, please remove the cobwebs from my mind, so that I can more clearly contemplate your love." The next week was the same, and the week after that, and the one after that! It was always: "Dear Lord, please remove the cobwebs from my mind so that I can more clearly contemplate your love."

Then one week, as this precious woman began her routine prayer, an exasperated sigh was heard from one of the other ladies. She interrupted the prayer with "God Almighty, just get rid of the spider!"

— Sandra Divnick

Recently relocated from Essex Junction, Vermont, writer Sandra Divnick lives on South Padre Island, Texas and is working towards a master's degree in elementary music education from the University of Texas at Brownsville.

My Evil Brother Was a Saint

There were two evil brothers. They were rich and used their money to keep their immoral ways from the public eye. They even attended the same church and, outwardly, looked to be perfect Catholics.

One day, their old pastor retired and a new one arrived. The new pastor saw right through the brothers' hypocrisy. Being a holy and dynamic man of God, he reinvigorated the parish and brought many people back to the Church. As the congregation grew, a fundraising campaign was started to build an addition onto the church.

Suddenly, one of the brothers died. The remaining brother sought out the new pastor the day before his brother's funeral and handed him a large check. "This is to complete the addition, Father," he explained.

"There is only one condition," he continued. "At the funeral, you must say brother was a saint." The pastor promised that he would and accepted the check.

The next day, Father began his homily and did not hold back: "He was an evil man. He cheated on his wife and abused his family." After going on in a similar vein for a few minutes, he finally concluded with, "But, compared to his brother, he was a saint!"

Apocalypse Now!

"Will we get out of school on Judgment Day?"

The Easy Way to Heaven

Want to get to heaven? Here's a little advice. It's easy to remember:

1. Be a coward
2. Cheat often.
3. Steal if you possibly can.

With a little effort, you could become a first-class cheatin', thievin' chicken.

Be a coward.

You want to be a coward because you're lazy and you're weak. (Do not start getting defensive. So am I.) Not only is it all right to admit these flaws, it is good to take full advantage of them when it comes to getting to heaven.

Why? First of all, there is a heaven. (Good.) Unfortunately, this means there is a hell, too. (Uh oh.)

Among the residents of hell are the angels who chose it—those who at some point in some way seriously rebelled against God. Their head honcho is Satan. You've probably heard of Satan. You've probably heard *from* Satan.

It is easier to get to heaven if you fervently believe there is a hell and there is a Satan and there are demons. That's so because Satan and other fallen angels want you to choose hell by also seriously rebelling against God. They want you to tell your Creator, "Go away. Leave me alone." God, being infinitely generous, lets human beings choose. And God honors each person's request. So where does this "be a chicken" business fit in?

Satan is oh-so-good at making rebellion look oh-so-attractive. That is the case even though rebelling against God is rebelling against who and what you truly are: a child of God created to spend eternity with God in heaven. The common name for rebelling—in big or little ways—is sin. The common name for marketing that rebellion—for making it seem like such a jim-dandy idea—is temptation. Before you sin, before anyone sins, there is temptation.

Sometimes fighting temptation by fighting temptation is foolish. It isn't that you're overmatched; you have God on your side. But why fight when you can run? That is where cowardice—"being a chicken"—is a virtue. Why prolong temptation when you can head for the hills? While it's true you can't permanently escape temptation here on earth, you can hightail it from what's being suggested right here and right now. Say a prayer and get out of there!

Cheat often.

Cheating is an art. In school, it has several tried-and-true variations. There is the penning of tiny uh ... reminders on one's palm just before a test. Or the desperate whispered plea to a nearby friend. And then there's the elaborate act that tells the world. "Oops, I dropped my pencil. I'm just picking it up."

In this life, humans are frequently tested. Ever notice how your life seems better when you give the correct answer? But what if you do not know the answer?

Cheat. Cheat. Cheat. On one palm, pen the Ten Commandments. On the other, the eight Beatitudes. Why? Because, in a nutshell, those are the answers. More than a list of rules and a set of recommendations, they are the carpenter's square, level, and plumb line in a skewed world. It's Christ's redemption that makes it possible to live these answers, to choose them, in this temptation-riddled world.

A fundamental of successful cheating is whispering to the person who has the right answer. Ask for help. From God, from Jesus, from the Holy Spirit. From the angels. From Mary and the saints. From family, friends, and our parish friends, both living and dead. Drop your pencil, lean over and scan what others have written. In Scripture. In the writings of the Church Doctors. In the writings and prayers of the saints. In the documents of the Church. In solid Catholic books and magazines and newspapers.

Steal if you possibly can.

Technically, you're only "'borrowing" because there is no copyright on sanctity. No patent on holiness. So take what you can from Mary, the saints, and the angels. The good men and women who have been a part of your own life (or are a part of it still). Become more like them by imitating what they did and how they did it.

Through the Communion of Saints—the souls in heaven and purgatory united with the faithful on earth—you can ask for help. You can turn to them. You can seek out and receive their friendship. Like Jesus, they love a good thief. They are delighted when a cowardly, cheating, stealing soul moves a step forward. Every step on that path is one step closer to paradise.

— Bill Dodds

Bill Dodds and his wife, Monica, are the editors of My Daily Visitor *magazine. Bill's latest books are* The Seeker's Guide to the Holy Spirit *(Loyola Press) and* Your One-Stop Guide to the Sacraments *(Servant Publications). To learn more about Bill's endeavors, visit www.BillDodds.com.*

Parishoners in Paradise

"It never occured to me that we would
still have to attend church."

It's All in the Name

I was teaching CCD class for my small country parish. The lesson for the day was on Moses. The kids listened, spellbound, to the story about baby Moses sent afloat in a basket. I explained Moses' childhood in the palace, his discovery that he was an Israelite, and his eventual fleeing into the desert. The kids listened with keen interest as I told them that Moses, while in the desert, took off his sandals and approached the burning bush from which God spoke and revealed His name, *Yahweh*. Seeing the kids' fascination with this story from Exodus, I was satisfied that it had been a good class. As I always did before dismissing them, I reviewed the day's lesson.

"Now what was the name God revealed to Moses at the burning bush?" I asked. One little girl waved her arm excitedly. "I know the answer!" she announced confidently. Her enthusiastic display made it impossible not to let her answer.

When I called on her she jumped up. "It's Yahoo!" she announced confidently.

Well, not quite. But I bet God wouldn't mind hearing a few "Yahoo's" when we call out His name.

— Susan Braun

Susan Braun is the proud mother of eight children. The Brauns recently moved back to the family farm in McVille, North Dakota that Susan grew up on when she was a kid.

In the Beginning, There Was No Duct Tape

God created the world before Home Depot existed. That's a theological concept I cannot comprehend. I take at least five trips to Home Depot during every project. The first trip is to buy materials, the second to return what I purchased and get the correct items, the third is to ask questions, the fourth because I forgot the answers, and the fifth to ask if I can pay someone to do the project for me.

Obviously, God is a better creator than I am. God created the entire universe. I can barely assemble a gas grill. Frankly, I have never completed a project and said, "It is good."

There are thousands of ways my ability to create pales in comparison to God's. For instance, during the creation of the world, God separated the light from the darkness. I have separated my children when they fight, but that's about it. God called the light Day, and the darkness He called Night. I called my neighbor to borrow a metric wrench to assemble the grill. God created "swarms of living creatures." I paid an exterminator $189 to get them out of my basement.

If I had created the world, my first words would have been, "Let there be duct tape to keep the stars from falling out of the sky and the leaves on the trees." Not God. His project was free of artificial adhesives. In my view, that's more miraculous than creating man from dust.

Not once during the six days did God have to go back and fix what he messed up the previous day. That raises the theological question, "Did God have instructions when creating the world?" Some Scripture scholars believe God had instructions but didn't read them, proving God is a man. Other scholars argue that God cannot be a man because there were no leftover parts on the sixth day when the project was completed. I'm no Bible expert, but if God is a man, I doubt He would have started the project in the first place. God created the world "in the beginning." Men never start a project in the beginning but rather wait for their wives to ask four or five times.

I have discovered two ways that I resemble the Creator. First, it takes me the same amount of time to assemble a gas grill that it took God to create the world: six days. Second, God rested on the seventh day. My wife says when it comes to napping, not even God is better than me.

— Tim Bete

Tim Bete's award-winning humor column has appeared in the Christian Science Monitor *and many parenting magazines. His first book,* Five Loaves, Two Fish – What, No Tartar Sauce?! (Minor Miracles in the Life of a Faith-Filled Father), *will be published by Sun Creek Books in Spring 2004. You can read more of Tim's work at www.TimBete.com*

God versus Darwin

One day, a group of Darwinian scientists got together and decided that man had come a long way and no longer needed God. So they picked out one Darwinian to go and tell God that they were done with Him.

The Darwinian walked up to God and said, "God, we've decided that we no longer need you. We're to the point that we can clone people and do many miraculous things, so why don't you just go and get lost."

God listened very patiently and kindly to the man. After the Darwinian was done talking, God said, "Very well, how about this? Let's say we have a man-making contest." To which the Darwinian happily agreed.

God added, "Now, we are going to do this just like I did back in the old days with Adam."

The Darwinian said, "Sure, no problem," and bent down and grabbed himself a handful of dirt.

God looked at him and said, "No, no, no. Go and make your own dirt!"

A Fish out of Water?

"That shouldn't be necessary, Noah."

Last Rites

A terrible strain of flu swept through the schools this year and caused the absentee lists to explode. My thirteen-year-old daughter, Amanda, was one of the casualties. After missing a week of class at her Catholic school, she returned six days later in time for their Friday school Mass.

Amanda's class was situated in the front pew facing the altar. She stood but then began to feel woozy from the overheated church air and the close quarters of more than six hundred students. Suddenly, she passed out cold, hitting her cheek on the kneeler. The priest rushed from the altar, as he had a clear view of her. With teachers, priest, and classmates crowded around her, she was shaken awake by a teacher. Cracking her eyes open slowly, at first only the priest's face came into view.

"Mama, I was sooo scared when I came to and saw Fr. Mark standing over me!" she explained in the car after I gathered her from school.

"Oh no! Did you think he was giving you last rites?" I asked.

"No, Mom, I thought he was going to give me mouth-to-mouth!"

— Angie Ledbetter

Angie Ledbetter writes from Baton Rouge, Louisiana.

The Atheist

An atheist was walking through the woods, admiring all the "accidents" that evolution had created. "What majestic trees! What powerful rivers! What beautiful animals!" he said to himself. As he was walking alongside the river, he heard a rustling in the bushes behind him.

Turning to look, he saw a seven-foot grizzly bear charge towards him. He ran as fast as he could up the path. He looked over his shoulder and saw the grizzly closing in. Somehow he ran even faster, so scared that tears came to his eyes. He looked again and the bear was even closer. His heart was pounding faster and he tried to run even faster still. He tripped and fell to the ground. He rolled over to pick himself up, but the bear was right beside him, reaching for him with its left paw and raising its right paw to strike him.

At that instant the atheist cried out, "Oh, my God!"

Immediately, time stopped ... the bear froze ... the forest was silent ... even the river stopped flowing.

As a bright light shone upon the man, a voice came from out of the sky. "You have denied My existence all these years, but do you now believe in Me?"

"No, I don't," replied the man, "but perhaps you could make the bear a believer?"

"Very well" said the voice.

The light went out ... the river ran again ... the sounds of the forest resumed ... and the bear dropped his right paw, brought both paws together, bowed his head and spoke ...

"Lord, bless this food which I am about to receive."

Chapter 5

His Healing Touch

Through the Wounds of Christ

They came as much to touch as to be touched. More than one thousand people—young and old, firm and infirm—flooded into the small sanctuary of Saints Cyril and Methodius Church in Sterling Heights, Michigan.

They waited in line for hours—some more than four-and-a-half hours—so that Francis, who bears the stigmata, could lay hands on them and pray over them. And much like St. Francis of Assisi, who also bore the wounds of Christ, this unassuming man does nothing on his own to draw attention to himself. Still the multitude came, many with tears streaming even before standing face-to-face with the man who bears wounds like those of Christ on his hands. They touched him and kissed his hands. A number were "slain in the spirit" and caught as they literally dropped at Francis' feet.

Some returned to tell others of the man with the healing touch, and more people came—even past midnight. That word-of-mouth communication is how most learned of Francis. While numerous physical and spiritual healings have been reported after contact with this humble, otherwise-ordinary man, he remains obedient to his spiritual advisors in shunning publicity and agreed to a brief interview only to benefit others.

Walter "Jack" Casey, an ex-policeman, was appointed by the bishop in Francis' diocese to travel with him. "He (the bishop) did not want me to be alone—ever," said Francis, the seventy-four-year-old devoutly Catholic Michigan man who is a father, grandfather, and great-grandfather.

"On Ash Wednesday in 1993 he was asked by Jesus if he would accept suffering, and forty days later the stigmata appeared," Casey said. "On Good Friday, the swelling on the top and bottom of his hands broke open and bled profusely."

Casey further explained that every morning, sometime between the hours of midnight and 3 a.m., 365 days a year, Francis suffers the passion of Christ. He suffers for the conversion of sinners and for those who have gone away from the sacraments to return.

"Our Blessed Mother has come to him nineteen times," Casey said. "Seven of those times she has told him, 'I will bring my people to you and you to my people.'"

Francis, who spoke only briefly, explained, "Jesus said to me, 'Use my hands to touch my people.'"

"I ask Jesus to put His healing hands on all of you. I know there are going to be healings and it might not be tonight, but something is going to happen to you. Please don't say, 'Francis healed me'; say, 'The Lord healed me. He is the only Healer. He is the only One'."

Fr. Robert J. Fox, founder of the Fatima Family Apostolate in South Dakota, has written a book about the Michigan man, *Francis*. "I felt it was important to explain the spirituality behind all this because a charism is not for oneself, but for others," Fr. Fox said. "A charism is a 'gift of grace' described by St. Paul in chapters twelve and fourteen of his first letter to the Corinthians."

Fr. Fox has been with Francis during and after his intense suffering. "His hands are extended up high as on the cross," Fr. Fox recounted. "After he has been some time in suffering, I see his hands slowly come down and rest on his chest. But the fact that he is still breathing is scarcely perceptible. I got very scared the first time I was with him and thought he had died. He was actually in ecstasy."

While there have been healings associated with Francis and documented in Fr. Fox's book, the priest is careful to point out that even amazing healings cannot be considered a supernatural miracle if there has been even one modern medical treatment.

Francis' humility and acceptance of the direction of his bishop are also a powerful testimony to his authenticity. In a letter to Fr. Fox, the bishop wrote, "I can find no fault with the activity that he is exercising. It seems to be helpful to many people. I was happy to give him my blessing." Francis keeps no money given or sent to him. "He doesn't accept a penny," said Fr. Fox.

But just how does this elderly gentleman stand for five or six hours without even sitting down? "The Lord protects me and I don't get tired," Francis explained. "Our Lord gave me this," he added, exposing his hands with the purple-black blotches on his palms. "He's protecting me."

— Diane Morey Hanson

Diane Morey Hanson writes magazine and newspaper articles from her home in Canton, Michigan. Diane is currently working with Ignatius Press on the autobiography of Alex Jones, a Pentecostal minister who entered the Catholic Church along with his family and fifty-three members of his congregation.

Fr. Robert Fox's book, Francis, *can be ordered through the Fatima Family Apostolate. Call (800) 213-5541. (Note: Francis is a fictitious name used to protect the identity of the man with the healing touch.)*

Unexpected Miracle

Five years after the miraculous events in her family's life, Kathy Crombie still can't talk about it without breaking down in tears—the events are so incredible to her. While seeking healing for her son's cancer, the miracle she personally experienced took her completely by surprise.

One day in August 1995, Chad Crombie, who had graduated from Dearborn High School in Michigan the previous spring, came home and told his parents that he had a lump on the side of his neck. "I wasn't feeling bad," Chad recalls, "so I didn't think much of it."

But for his parents, Kathy and Robyn Crombie, what they hoped was a swollen gland turned out to be their worst nightmare. "The doctor came out and said it was cancer," said Kathy, forty-eight. "Holy smokes, it hit us so hard." They had found two lumps and Chad was diagnosed with Hodgkin's lymphoma. The course of treatment decided on was a rigorous forty rounds of radiation—twenty to the upper body and twenty to the lower body.

"You suddenly find God," Kathy explained. "I was raised Catholic and my parents were very good role models. I continued to go to church and my husband converted when we married, but I had issues with the Church. I was a marginal Catholic—confession wasn't high on my priority list, the Rosary was a mindless prayer and the Church was outdated on the contraception thing."

So when one of Kathy's best friends called with a suggestion, it totally blew her away.

Judy Paga told Kathy she knew of a man in Michigan, named Francis, who had the wounds of Christ in his hands. Judy urged her to take Chad to him. "I expect nothing less than a miracle," she told Kathy.

"I felt so confused," Kathy said. After gathering her thoughts, Kathy said, she presented the information to her family. She asked Chad, who had undergone his first four radiation treatments, if he wanted to go.

To her surprise he answered, "Oh, sure, Mom."

"I didn't even know what a stigmatist was," Chad confessed. "I never had any doubts that God exists and is still in the miracle-working business. My practical side said, 'Go,' what do you have to lose?" Still, Kathy hesitated, "We really need to talk to someone who knows about this."

Kathy decided to check with her pastor of twenty-five years, Msgr. Herman Kucyk, at Divine Child Parish in Dearborn. "Monsignor is an incredible priest," she said. When Msgr. Kucyk said he had never heard of the man, Kathy remembers asking, "'Gee, Father, what should we do?' I don't know what I was hoping to hear."

What she heard was, "Oh, I'd go! I'd go in a minute. I believe that God gives special gifts to people. While you're there, you'll know if he is real. And if he is, ask him to come to our church sometime—we have a lot of sick people who could use his services."

Msgr. Kucyk later said, "At that time, they needed all the prayer they could get. I thought, if he could help, all the better."

"He is the reason we went," Kathy said. "God truly used him that day. If he had said no, we wouldn't have gone." On Saturday, October 21st, Kathy and Chad drove to Flint where Francis—the man with the wounds of Christ—was visiting his brother Reynold. Chad's older brother Derek was playing football for Wayne State that day and his father had injured his back; neither could make the 10 a.m. appointment. When they came into the family room there were a few other people listening to Francis' explanation of his wounds.

"All of a sudden I see his hands with these huge wounds on the palms—about the size of a silver dollar," Kathy remembered. "They are these deep, deep purple-red, scabbed-over wounds. On the back of his hands were band-aids and you could see blood under them."

He explained that every night he suffers the passion of our Lord, for the sins of the flesh, sometime between the hours of midnight and 3 a.m. "He told us, that is the time when a great deal of the sins of the flesh are committed," said Kathy. When he began to explain the suffering, "He broke down crying like I have never heard anyone else cry."

After Francis regained his composure, Reynold told those gathered that his brother would pray with them in a separate room if they wished. "A man went in first and I was kind of relieved," said Kathy. "I didn't know what to make of it all."

Chad volunteered to go next and was in there for quite some time. "We prayed and he puts his hands on my head," Chad recounted. "I got a chill that felt more electric than cold. It shot straight through and I felt completely relaxed."

When he came out, Kathy went in. Francis told her that she didn't need to pray out loud because God would hear her prayer. "I totally felt I was in God's hands," said Kathy. "I remember crying like a baby. I couldn't stop. It was a feeling I will never forget. I had never experienced anything like that in my life."

Kathy said that when she and Chad got into the car she was still crying. She reached into her pocket to grab a tissue Francis had given her in the house. "I went to wipe my eye and I caught a whiff of something perfumy," she said. "I don't wear perfume because I'm allergic to it." She checked the tissue and there was no lotion on it. "Then I smelled my hands and it was on my hands and Chad's hands too. It was very flowery—like roses. At that time, I didn't know about roses being a sign of Mary."

"It smelled like a whole flower shop," Chad added, "it was so strong." The mother and son didn't have much time to ponder the scent (which continued into the next day) because of what happened next. "We were about five minutes down the road," recalled Chad, who added that he was in the habit of frequently feeling his neck. "I had checked the lump that morning and it was huge, even larger than it had been before. About the time we first smelled the roses my hand automatically went across my neck.

"I felt again and it began to register that the lump was not there. I said, 'Mom, it's gone,' and she said, 'What's gone?' I said, 'The lump is gone.'" As soon as the Crombies arrived home, Kathy and Robyn checked Chad for any sign of the tumor. "The lump was definitely gone," said Kathy. Five years later, Chad has no signs of Hodgkin's.

As miraculous as Chad's healing was to the Crombies, Kathy was shocked by her own personal healing. "God physically healed Chad, but He gave me a spiritual conversion I didn't even know I needed," she said. Once a marginal Catholic, Kathy is now a daily Communicant and also prays the rosary every day. "I shortchanged all of my family because of my skepticism," Kathy confessed.

"I wasn't solid in my faith and I was so verbal about it. People who see me now say, 'Boy, have you changed.'"

And the changes weren't limited just to Kathy. "I watched my husband grow in his faith. I watched my boys grow in their faith so incredibly. I see in them such strong Catholics."

Chad is very aware of the impact all this has had on his spiritual life. "I have always been strong in my belief, but it is completely cemented now," he said. For the Crombie family, the greatest miracle has definitely been their conversion of faith.

"God has done this for others to witness," said Kathy. "And this is for everyone."

— Diane Morey Hanson

See Diane's biography after Through the Wounds of Christ *at the beginning of this chapter.*

Gone but Not Forgotten

Taking a deep breath, I exhaled slowly, trying to breathe through the pain. Something was terribly wrong. It was 1957 and I was pregnant with our sixth child. I was twenty-seven and my five children were all under the age of eight. It was a busy time, but the news that I was expecting another child brought only joy to my husband, John, and me. "Another precious gift from God," we thought.

The pregnancy began like the others, with morning sickness that felt like the three-month flu. It was just beginning to subside at twelve weeks like the others had, when I began bleeding. This had happened during another pregnancy which had ended in a healthy baby. Still, I was concerned, especially when I began feeling a dull pain in my abdomen. I went to my doctor right away.

After the examination, my doctor's somber face told the story. "I think you are going to miscarry," he said gently. My throat swelled as I tried to swallow back the tears. I already loved this baby.

"He could be wrong," I thought. "I'll go home and rest like I did the last time. Maybe things will get better."

By morning, the pain, both physical and emotional, was unbearable. I knew I was losing the baby. My husband called a neighbor to come stay with me so I would not be alone while he left to work at the paper mill. By then I was terrified. "Please God, if there is any way, save my baby," I prayed. Still, I trusted enough in God to accept His will if he chose to call my baby home. But the pain, was increasing. Even praying became difficult.

The knife-like cramping and bleeding was draining me of my strength. Was I dying too?

My neighbor insisted I call the doctor. Those were the days when doctors made house calls. He was busy but informed me he would try to get to my house by noon. It was only 9 a.m. I mustered all my strength and replied. "If you cannot come here and take care of me now, I need to get a doctor that will."

The doctor arrived in fifteen minutes. It was then that he realized I had an ectopic pregnancy. The baby was not planted in my womb but had been growing in my fallopian tube, which was now ruptured. An ambulance came and sped me to the hospital.

I breathed slowly and prayed through the pain. "Surely, I must be dying," I thought. "Please, someone get me a priest," I begged. I wanted to receive the sacrament of confession before going into surgery. I wanted to be ready to meet God. There was a bit of confusion at first but finally a priest came and heard my confession. "There," I thought in my painful stupor. "I am ready now."

Blinking open my eyes in the recovery room I focused on the tubes coming out of my arm. A pint of blood hung alongside me replacing some of the massive amount I had lost. The realization of what had happened stabbed my heart. I was still alive, praise be to God, but my baby was gone. A profound sense of emptiness enveloped me. "My baby ... " I sobbed to a nurse at my side.

"You are very sick," she explained calmly. "You've lost a lot of blood but you will be fine soon." Anytime I began to show grief over my lost baby, someone quickly quieted me insisting I would be just fine. The message came through loud and clear: You have five children at home. This was only a twelve-week baby. There is no reason for tears.

After ten days in the hospital, I returned home to care for my family. The doctor warned against another pregnancy, but I had the joy of another beautiful baby five years later. Life was busy and good. The whole episode became buried into the recesses of my mind for thirty years. But then, without warning, the memory forced its way out of dormancy.

Sitting at my dining room table writing up a speech for an upcoming Cursillo weekend retreat, I began with all the usual background information about myself. It was natural to begin with my family. "I have six children," I wrote.

Without warning, a voice from within corrected me. *No, you have seven children.* I honestly think it was Our Lady speaking to me. The voice was so gentle and so true. I sat at the table, stunned. I put down my pen. The words echoed in my brain: *You have seven children.*

"I have seven children. I have seven children," I thought, again and again. For thirty years I had ignored the existence of a child of mine. Like a dam bursting forth, tears flooded down my face. "My baby," I thought, "My precious baby is in heaven with God."

I put my speech aside, unable to focus on what I should say. For several days I allowed myself the luxury of grieving the loss of my baby so long ago. If people thought I was wrong to cry over it at the time, I could only imagine what they would think of all my tears thirty years later.

Around this time, I went for coffee at a newly opened senior social center for people fifty-five and older. I was fifty-seven. A lady, who I recognized as working at the hospital years earlier, joined me at my table.

She studied me carefully then her face lit up with recognition. "Oh! I know who you are," she declared. "You are the woman who had the ectopic pregnancy." I was so surprised. Why would she remember me after all these years? "I have always wanted to tell you," she said, "I baptized your baby."

I was speechless. Now my tears were tears of joy. Only God could have arranged such a meeting at just the right moment in my life. Peace and calm filled me. Finally, I was ready to go home and finish my speech. But first, I had one more thing to do. I named my little boy: David Benjamin, my little angel whom I look forward to meeting one day in heaven.

— Agnes L'Heureux

Agnes L'Heureux loves to share her faith. This seventy-two-year-old mother of six grown children, fourteen grandchildren, and one great-grandchild has been involved in various types of evangelization since 1979. Agnes currently works from her home in International Falls, Minnesota, for a books-on-tape ministry.

My Day to Plant

Because I fly often, I have been able to meet many interesting people on planes. I usually look for opportunities to get to know people and, if possible, to share my faith in Christ with them. Evangelists often refer to this as "planting seeds of faith."

One early morning as I was sitting in my seat waiting for the plane to take off, I noticed a young woman walk through the door of the aircraft. I'm sure everyone else in first class must have noticed her as well because she was a very striking lady. She took her seat next to mine and reached into her carry-on bag for her daily newspaper.

As she opened her newspaper I greeted her with a cheerful, "Hello. Is Minneapolis your home or are you traveling?" Before she could answer, several huge men of monster proportions stepped onto the plane. Like the striking young lady, you could not help but notice these men, as they were all close to seven feet tall and three hundred or more pounds.

"I'm here on business," Jane (not her real name) answered. "I work for the WWF, the World Wrestling Federation."

"Really?" I asked, now making sense out of the cast of characters boarding the plane. "So what kind of business are you in?"

"I'm one of the blonde bimbo managers that stands in the corner in a bikini," she replied, somewhat sarcastically.

Since I was not a regular fan of WWF, I had no way of placing her on that wrestling show, but I had an idea of what she was talking about.

After some small talk about the wrestling event the night before, there was a pause. So I asked her a point blank question and got to the heart of the matter. "So are you happy doing that?" I asked.

My question took her by surprise. Her expression changed from aloof to serious. "What do you mean?" she asked.

"I mean are you happy doing what you do?" I reiterated. "Is that what you've always wanted to do? I'm a Christian and I've always been curious if people involved in that sort of entertainment are truly happy."

Staring straight ahead, she paused for a long time, reflecting on the question. "No, I'm not," she finally answered. She proceeded to tell me that while working as a make-up artist for CNN, she was offered the WWF job. Recently divorced with a child, the opportunity to make more money was tempting. She related that what she had really wanted to do was to finish her education and pursue her relationship with Christ.

I expressed to her that she was part of an entertainment industry that is changing our culture negatively, and that it teaches our young men that women should be looked upon as sex objects.

With a look of sadness, Jane told me she was not proud of what she was doing. "I was raised a Baptist and loved the Lord," she explained. "I have not been living for Him the way I used to. This is not what I planned to do with my life."

"God has a plan for your life," I told her. "He has a way for you to walk with Him. You don't have to do this."

We talked from the time we left Minneapolis until we landed in Atlanta. I suggested that perhaps God was using WWF's coming to Minneapolis as an opportunity for us to have this conversation. I could tell by her expression that she was deeply moved by what I had said.

I wish I could say she made a decision that day about her future, but I cannot. Since Scripture tells us that one man plants, another man waters, and God causes the increase, all I could do was plant a seed or water a previously planted seed. Perhaps I was watering that day.

People often ask me, "Why do these kinds of things always happen to you?" I tell them things like this happen to everyone who asks God to use them. I am totally convinced that God is involved in our daily lives and that He desires to use us as His instruments of hope, healing, and good news, if we will only allow Him.

— Jeff Cavins

The Making of a Saint

What kind of family refuses the offer of spiritual intervention for a crippled daughter? A very rare and selfless one, as it turns out.

"We had offered to make a novena to our foundress, Mother Leonie Aviat, on several occasions. But the McKenzie family turned it down," said Sister Anne Elizabeth Eder of the Oblate Sisters of St. Francis de Sales in Drexel Hill, Pennsylvania. She was the principal of the elementary school attended by Bernadette McKenzie Kutufaris.

Mother Aviat was a co-founder of the religious order that eventually spread its charitable work to Europe, South Africa, and Ecuador. She died on January 10, 1914, leaving the precept: "Let us work for the happiness of others."

"The sisters approached us several times about the novena," said Denise McKenzie, Bernadette's mother. "But until the third surgery, we felt that there was always hope. We felt that there was another child in much worse condition than our daughter and it would be selfish to deprive another family who had no hope."

Bernadette was suffering from tethered spinal cord syndrome, a rare condition in which the base of the spine is shredded into tethers and the presence of fatty tumors prevents the spinal cord from keeping pace with the growth of the spine. The condition first presented itself in 1988 when Bernadette was ten.

Bernadette was referred to a neurosurgeon, who believed that once the tumors were removed the pain would end. The surgery, which was supposed to last four hours, took almost seven. Things were much worse than originally thought. The tumors had grown intertwined with her nerves. Her agony continued.

Along with the physical pain came the social isolation that kids often experience from their peers. "The kids weren't overtly mean," Sister Anne Elizabeth said, "but Bernadette wasn't included in many of the normal activities." With a laugh, Bernadette recalls, "When I couldn't go to school, Sister Anne would bring me 'important' files to work on. That made me feel worthwhile and useful. It wasn't until years later I discovered it was just busy work to keep my morale up."

But there was precious little laughter as the condition worsened. "There was never a moment that I didn't feel pain to some degree," Bernadette remembers.

After two initial surgeries, the pain resumed. Bernadette began high school in 1990. A year later, a third surgery was performed. After this operation, she was not even able to make it to physical therapy. When the family visited Dr. Bruce Northrup of Thomas Jefferson University Hospital, they went expecting to hear plans for a fourth surgery. "He asked Bernadette to leave the room," Denise said. "The doctor told us that our daughter was a surgical failure. He referred us to a pain specialist because Bernadette was going to be bedridden and in chronic pain for the rest of her life. Paralysis was also a concern. In fact, the doctors were amazed that she could still feel her legs at this point."

Bernadette was devastated. "I needed my parents for everything now," she said, "to help me walk, to get dressed. I used to cry at night, asking someone up there to make me better. When that didn't happen, my faith and belief in God were really gone."

One particular piece of bad news was like a dagger in the heart for Bernadette. She would never dance again. Dancing meant the world to her.

During her darkest hour, a ray of divine light came shining through. Sister Anne Elizabeth approached the McKenzies again with the novena proposal. "It's time we storm heaven," she told them. This time the family accepted the offer.

Father Shaun Mahoney, the associate pastor at St. Bernadette parish at the time, was conducting Sunday evening adoration and benediction. The novena began on March 22, 1992, led by this prayer group. "We placed novena cards in the church pews ahead of time," says Father Mahoney. The prayer effort spread to a wider audience beyond the parish. Novena booklets were distributed to every student in the girls and the adjoining boys' high schools. The novena ended up involving more than two-thousand people.

In order for a person to be canonized a Catholic saint, two miracles credited to the intercession of the holy person must be verified. In 1991, Pope John Paul II proclaimed Mother Aviat's first miracle, when she was credited with saving the severely burned and infected right arm of Vincent Kesner, a South African boy, in 1976. Now the people in this Philadelphia suburb were praying for a second miracle.

Confined to bed, Bernadette fervently prayed for Mother Aviat's intercession. But things got worse before they got better. "The night before the miracle I was up all night in the worst pain I ever experienced," Bernadette says. "Later on I found out that many recipients of miracles experience their worst agony right before the healing."

The next day, March 25th, was the last day of the novena. Bernadette was left alone while her parents and four siblings were busy elsewhere. Bernadette has no memory of anything from ten o'clock in the morning until two in the afternoon that day. "When I came to, I didn't feel any pain," Bernadette said. Contrary to what one might expect, the fourteen-year-old was not overwhelmed.

"When the novena started, everything changed for me. It wasn't a matter of if but when I would get better," said Bernadette.

She started walking around in circles and then throughout the house. When her parents returned home, they were shocked. That night, Bernadette had dinner with her family and then washed the dishes—simple acts which many take for granted, but extraordinary ones for a person whose life had been a prison of pain.

Word began to get out. Bernadette's parents called Sister Anne Elizabeth. "It was an overwhelming sense of the awesome power of prayer when I heard of the miracle," Sister said, "When people join together, prayers can be answered."

When Denise called the high school to tell them Bernadette would be returning, the news swept forth like a tidal wave, eventually making its way to the Vatican. It looked as if Bernadette's miracle would be the one that moved Mother Aviat from "Blessed" to "Saint."

After significant scientific study and theological review, the review board made its recommendation to the pope. Then on December 18, 2000, Pope John Paul II declared Bernadette's cure a miracle.

Bernadette said, "I went from asking, 'Why me? Why am I sick?' to 'How much can I give back?'" She did a lot of traveling and missionary work. At age nineteen, she worked in an impoverished town in Mexico, teaching and distributing clothes and repairing homes. For two years she also worked with tribes in San Fidel, New Mexico, teaching career development and sign language.

Bernadette has gone on to get her bachelor's and master's degrees. On September 14, 2001, she married Andrew Kutufaris. She danced at her wedding.

Today, she delights in telling the story of her miracle, and spreading a message of faith and hope.

— Joseph M. O'Loughlin

Joseph M. O'Loughlin is a freelance writer and columnist who is a regular contributor to news publications of the greater Philadelphia area. His work has appeared in St. Anthony Messenger, Pray, Ministry Today, SportSpectrum, *and* CrossWalk.com. *In addition, Joseph writes regularly for* Baseball Digest, Basketball Digest, *and* Phillies Report.

The Gift of Quitting

I began smoking in 1960 when I was just twelve years old. By sixteen, I was given permission to smoke in the house. I am one of those people who does things in excess, so it was not long before I was smoking two packs a day.

In my forties, I got breast cancer and had a mastectomy. The first thing I wanted after surgery was a cigarette. During my entire stay in the hospital, I spent much of my time going downstairs and outside for cigarettes. I went through eight and a half grueling months of chemotherapy but still did not quit smoking.

When I was about forty-five, I had to get by on disability payments with no child support for my three children. Yet, somehow I still found the money for my cigarettes. As Christmas approached, I was flat broke and very depressed. Fortunately, one of the local churches sponsored families for Christmas and we were picked, so my children would have presents after all. I was extremely grateful, but I was still not in a festive mood. I did not have the heart for our traditional Advent preparations that year.

On Christmas morning, my little boy asked me what I was giving the Baby Jesus for His birthday. I was crushed as I had nothing. I had not baked our customary birthday cake for baby Jesus, nor had we stored up our good deeds to fill the manger with straw, like in years past. I felt bad but the look on my son's face told me he felt worse. The next thing out of my mouth surprised even me.

"I know," I said impulsively. "I am giving Baby Jesus my smoking habit. The whole thing: the cigarettes, the lighters, the cravings, the crabbiness, the ashtrays both dirty and clean, everything about smoking is what I am giving to Baby Jesus."

He was delighted and ran to tell his sister. They were filled with such joy while I sat stunned at what I had just done. I was obsessed with cigarettes yet I had just told my son that I was giving up smoking as a gift to the Baby Jesus. Was I nuts? Could I do it?

"No way," I thought. But I knew that to break such a promise to my son would haunt us both for years to come. I needed a miracle. "Look Jesus," I prayed. "I am sorry for jumping the gun, but I made this promise to my child. Now I need You to help me keep it."

Suddenly I was filled with a deep sense of sureness. The kids and I had a ball going from room to room collecting everything to do with cigarettes. There were packs hidden everywhere—five in the freezer alone. We took the cigarettes, lighters, and ashtrays and either gave or threw them away. Then I went from room to room taking down curtains and cleaning them. I washed walls, ceilings, clothing and everything I could find, from Christmas morning until well into the new year.

Each time I saw a smoker, I privately thanked God for taking away my habit. Then, I asked Him to do the same for them. I do that to this day. It has been nine years and I have never had so much as a single craving.

That was the year of my Christmas miracle and it changed my life completely. I learned that when we step out in faith everything is possible with God. I saw firsthand what Jesus meant when He spoke about having faith the size of a mustard seed.

I gave up smoking as a gift to Baby Jesus, but in turn it was a gift He gave to me.

— Dani D'Angelo

Dani D'Angelo is the mother of one adult daughter, two teenagers, and the grandmama of two little ones. By working at the Hebron House of Hospitality in Waukesha, Wisconsin, which maintains three homeless shelters, Dani is able to encourage and assist women in need by helping them to obtain employment and housing. Her written work has appeared in Now and at the Hour *and her poetry has been published on several websites including 2theheart.com.*

Watch What You Pray For

Everyone has heard the saying: "Watch what you pray for, you may get it." When I was pregnant with our third child, I prayed that God would take my unborn baby before he was born. My husband, Mike, and I had two adorable children: six-year-old Abby-Lynn and four-year-old Cameron. We had room in our hearts for another child ... but just not this one, or so I thought.

Amniocentesis revealed that the little boy I carried had Down Syndrome, a heart defect, and other possible major anomalies. The news hit me like a sledge hammer. For some reason, ever since I was a child, I had a deep fear that one day I would have a Down child. I'm ashamed to admit it but I feared Down children and turned away from them.

My heart cried with love for my poor disabled baby. I truly did love him. It was just beyond my ability to cope, I thought. "Lord, please take this little angel. This is more than I can handle," I prayed. The "glow" of motherhood turned into depression. I envisioned the birth of my baby as the beginning of a life-long struggle—a child that would be dependent on me the rest of my life.

Then at thirty-one weeks two different neonatal specialists told us that the baby was swelling with fluid in major organs, a medical disorder called "non-immune hydrops" that was "incompatible with life." His body cavity was filled with fluid. His scalp, heart, lungs, chest, abdomen, kidneys, and scrotum were all filled with fluid. It was basically a fatal condition. The ultrasound showed the fluid, and the testing (by amniocentesis) backed it up.

The expectation was that he would die in utero within a week or two. This was what I had prayed for because I thought it was for the best.

Even if the baby were brought to term, the experts believed he would not live for more than a few minutes because the fluid buildup was so severe. The baby's lungs were compressed with fluid making it impossible to breathe on his own. The doctor wanted us to deliver the baby early so as to relieve me of the burden. I told the doctor that everything would be in God's hands. We then waited for the baby to die.

Three weeks later, the baby's heartbeat remained strong and his movement was constant, I wondered how he could be dying. I could feel him in my womb constantly kicking and moving. Then something began to happen that I had not anticipated. My baby became so alive and real to me, and I began to fall in love with him.

Suddenly, all the love of which I was capable welled up within me and cried out for my baby. I loved him so much and did not want him to die. Was God taking my baby because I did not have faith enough and love enough to believe I could care for him?

At this point, I would gladly accept the handicaps of my baby if only he would live. It was a wake-up call to the shallow faith I had been practicing. My selfishness hindered love of God and love of others and even love for my very own baby. For the first time in my life, I fully put myself in God's hands, whatever that meant. It was then that peace washed over me. "God, you alone know what is best for our family and our baby." I prayed. "I trust in You. Help that trust to grow." Now I was praying for two things: a miracle that my baby would live or peace of mind to accept God's will if he did not.

During the last two months, Mike and I made arrangements at a funeral home. In late August, two weeks before the baby's due date, I went into active labor. They put me in the last delivery room, all the way at the end. Everyone knew what was going to happen and they were ready for a heartbreaking night. Thankfully, I had one of the most beautiful nurses who comforted me. She gave me a prayer card of St. Gerard Majella, the patron saint of expectant mothers.

The instructions were that they would only make the baby comfortable until he passed. I went into emotional shutdown. I could not push because his birth would mean he would die. I did not want to let go of him. I cried more in that hour than I have cried in my lifetime. I prayed: "Just give me five minutes with him.'"

Our baby boy—Dustin Raphael Gary, 7 pounds, 10 ounces—was born alive, kicking and screaming. Mike baptized him immediately, thinking we might have only minutes with him. After ten minutes of screaming and crying the baby looked pink. The only thing purple were his hands and feet. I was expecting a baby who was dying. Then I heard a gurgling sound, and I thought to myself, "Oh, this is it." But they syringed out the fluid and his eyes started opening and he started rooting. I begged God, "Please don't take this baby from me."

Finally, we called for a pediatrician to examine the baby. He looked at the file and then looked at Dustin, then said: "This file and this child are not the same. There's no way. The file says he's incompatible with life.'"

The only place he had fluid was in one of his kidneys and his scrotum. I believe God healed him from the head down and stopped low enough to show that this wasn't a mistake—this was a miracle. He is a miracle. He would not be here if not for the grace of God.

I chose the name "Dustin" because it means "Fighter," and "Raphael" means "healed by God." He became the light of our family six months ago. Dustin has brought more love to us than we ever imagined. He has changed everything in my own life: my ability to love, to trust in God and to see miracles all around me.

He is the angel that was put here to bring us closer to God. I am thirty-five and I have never known God like I know Him now. Even my mom, who is sixty-seven, says she's never seen the Lord like she sees him now. I lived in a box before. Dustin has changed our world; he has brought God into it.

— Liz Gray

Liz Gray is the mother of three children. She also works closely with a Louisiana children's musician who helps keep her young at heart. When this musician told her how much he loves to work with kids with Down Syndrome, Liz never imagined that she would one day be the mother of one such beautiful child. She is amazed at how God brings people together in this world. The Gray family lives in Mandeville, Louisiana. To learn more about the children's musician with whom Liz works, go to www.papillion.com.

More Than I Asked

Looking at the day ahead of me, I was anxious to get the clutter of doctor's appointments out of the way. Although I felt in great health at the age of thirty-five, I figured it was about time to have my cholesterol and glucose levels checked. But first there was an appointment with the oral surgeon. My dentist had seemed unconcerned with the small sore at the back of my mouth, but like most doctors he had a "better to be safe than sorry" mind set. He referred me to an oral surgeon.

After examining the sore the previous week, the doctor had announced it looked like ulcerative tissue—nothing to worry about. But just to rule out anything serious, he took the standard biopsy. This morning's appointment was to go over the results.

"Oh well," I thought, "at least I squeezed both appointments early in the morning so I won't miss much work." As I sat in the waiting room, my mind became occupied with my job as an engineer with the Federal Aviation Administration in Minnesota.

"David Stefonowicz," the nurse called, interrupting my thoughts. Relieved that the wait had been short, I jumped up and followed her into the patient room. The doctor quickly came through the door and quietly closed it. His young face looked taut with strain. He looked me uncomfortably in the eyes.

"This is not the routine," I thought. "Something is wrong." I became flushed and my stomach sank like lead.

"The pathology report shows that you have cancer," the doctor said slowly but firmly. "Squamous cell carcinoma. It is a very aggressive type of cancer. We do not know how long you've had this or how far it has spread. This is very serious. I've set up an appointment for you this Friday to meet with a specialist, Dr. Adams, at the University of Minnesota."

Cancer. My ears heard clearly, but my brain froze, unable to absorb it. I listened, made note of my appointment, and asked a few questions. I thanked the doctor and numbly left his office in a dream-like state, headed to my next appointment. It was all surreal.

"Cancer," I thought as the nurse drew my blood. I watched the lab technicians, receptionists, and patients hustle about their business. I felt so far removed from them all. "I have cancer," the words rang in my head. "They are all going about their lives as usual, but my life is different now. I have cancer."

The good news that my glucose and cholesterol levels were normal seemed insignificant at this point. I drove home to my wife, Teri. She looked at my stricken face as I walked through the door knowing instantly that something was very wrong. "I have cancer," I told her immediately, and explained the situation.

In the embrace of my wife, my heart finally plugged into my brain, releasing a floodgate of tears. I did not feel alone anymore. We cried and hugged. As I held Teri, the cancer was no longer just about me; it was about Teri, my daughter, Brittany, age thirteen, and sons, Chris, and Benjamin, ages eleven and eight. They all needed me.

With Teri at my side, we told the kids. Then we all cried and prayed together. Looking into the faces of my loved ones, I became determined to do everything possible to beat this cancer. But I realized I could not do it alone. I needed God more than ever.

Teri called her brother, Fr. Wayne Sattler. He suggested I receive the sacrament of the anointing of the sick. He also said he would be praying for the intercession of Mother Teresa. While Fr. Wayne was in seminary in Rome, several meetings with Mother Teresa had inspired him to greater spirituality. Although she has not yet been canonized as a saint of the Church, Fr. Wayne believes her to be a powerful intercessor in heaven. He sent us prayer cards with prayers for her intercession.

We petitioned Mother Teresa daily to intercede with her prayers that my cancer would not spread and would be cured. Fr. Wayne asked his parishioners to include me in their prayers and to pray these cards on my behalf. He sent cards to all our family members and asked them too to pray for Mother Teresa's intercession.

We did not stop there. We asked everyone we knew to pray for healing. We prayed Rosaries, went to extra Masses and prayed unceasingly. Although I was determined to beat the cancer, I still had to face my mortality head on. My Internet research revealed a fifty percent survival rate five years after treatment for my kind of cancer. That put my life's odds on par with a coin toss.

I so desperately wanted my life to stay the same. My family needed me. "Please God," I prayed. "Let me live to take care of Teri and the kids."

I was also so full of anger and guilt. You see, I had chewed tobacco for fifteen years, despite Teri's pleas that I give it up. "How could I have been so stupid?" I wondered. "Why did I think it wouldn't be me with cancer?" I begged God to spare Teri and the kids from suffering as a result of my bad choices. My heartfelt prayers were more for the love of my family than for myself.

Two days after my diagnosis, on September 20, Teri and I celebrated our fourteenth year of marriage. While we basked in our years of holy union, neither of us were in the frame of mind for a "celebration." We walked in the woods hand-in-hand for over an hour. Then, we went to dinner but barely touched our food. The blessing of our years together was overshadowed by the threat that it could soon be over. We stopped at church on the way home to pray a Rosary together.

After my appointment with Dr. Adams and subsequent x-rays and scans, I received encouraging news. The tumor looked small. Dr. Adams spoke encouragingly about my chances for a cure. He explained that a limited procedure would remove three teeth and some supporting bone.

Although Dr. Adams was optimistic, he warned me that the full extent of the cancer would not be known until the surgery, which was two weeks away, on October 10, 2000.

Those two weeks seemed more like two months. Although I tried to remain upbeat, the fact that my cancer was such an aggressive type haunted me. Would the wait for surgery allow the cancer to spread and diminish my chances for survival? I tried to push those thoughts away. I had to trust in God. God decided such things. My job was to pray. I could not undo my years of using chewing tobacco. I could not ensure my survival. I could only wait, pray and trust in God.

I got to the hospital early for the 11:45 a.m. surgery, cautiously relieved the day had finally arrived. Teri and I hugged good-bye as I was wheeled away to the operating room. Three hours later, I woke up to excruciating pain. Shaking violently from the after affects of the anesthesia compounded the throbbing pain in my mouth and throat. Stitches, cotton and a plastic plate covering my mouth made it impossible to speak.

I wanted to know how the surgery went, but I could not form the question to ask the nurse. Not until I was wheeled from the recovery room to the patient room was I able to see Teri. She put her arms around me and kissed me. I looked into her eyes, waiting to hear how the surgery went. "Did they get it all? Has it spread?" I desperately wanted to know yet feared a negative response.

I had prayed so hard for a full recovery. I believed God could allow me to get better and I prayed that this would be His will. What He did, however, I had never asked for. It was more than I ever dreamed of.

"The doctor removed three teeth and quite a bit of tissue and bone at the site," Teri explained. "but Dave, the pathology test done in the surgery room showed no cancer."

Subsequent tests showed there was no trace of cancer. Baffled, Dr. Adams went back to the initial biopsy. The tissue was definitely cancerous. He re-examined the tissue removed during surgery. No cancer whatsoever.

My family and I sincerely believe that God healed my cancer through the intercession of Mother Teresa. Through the grace of God I have been blessed with a second chance and I will do everything possible to live each moment in union with Him now. He has given me more than I will ever deserve and more than I asked.

I later learned that at one of the meetings Fr. Wayne had with Mother Teresa, she had asked Fr. Wayne to pray for her and her mission. He readily agreed. She assured him that if he prayed for her and her mission now, she would pray for him when she was in heaven. During my ordeal, Fr. Wayne was pretty firm with Mother Teresa. He told her he had kept his end of the bargain and now he expected her to hold up her end. He depended on her prayers for me, his brother-in-law. We believe she was faithful to her word.

And so, now fully healed, I have presented my story for Mother Teresa's cause for sainthood to the postulator in Calcutta, India.

— David Stefanowicz

David Stefanowicz loves to spend time with his three children. When he's not busy at work for the Federal Aviation Administration, David coaches his kids' soccer, basketball, baseball, and softball teams. In addition to coaching, he enjoys bike riding and camping. David, his wife Teri, and their kids live in Lakeville, Minnesota.

Healed Heart

I now understand what the saying, "When it rains, it pours," really means. It was certainly true several months before my oldest daughter's wedding. Only in our case, it was not only pouring but storming.

Christine, my daughter, was hospitalized in a Chicago hospital for pneumonia. My husband, Mike, traveled from our home in Michigan to be with her. I stayed behind to care for my mother who had a stroke that same week. After five days in the hospital, Christine only grew worse.

It was at this time that Mike began having dizzy spells. A nurse sent him to the emergency room where he was diagnosed with high blood pressure and told to see his doctor when he returned home.

But just as in the Bible, when Jesus calmed the storm at sea, so He calmed our storm. In Jesus' presence, during perpetual adoration, I learned to trust and let Him calm all my storms. I gave Him all our struggles and He took care of them.

After a lung biopsy, Christine was finally given the proper medication and soon healed. My mother's condition also improved. And Mike, being his normal self, forgot about seeing his doctor, since he was feeling better. We all set our mind to preparing for Christine's August wedding.

Repeated dizzy spells, however, nagged Mike enough that he finally relented and went to his doctor. The diagnosis, atrial tachycardia, was a serious warning for a potential stroke. His heartbeat would climb to one hundred and fifty beats per minute. A procedure to treat it was ordered in May. It would take up to seven hours.

During the procedure our family prayed the rosary over and over, hoping to guide the surgeon's hands and heal my husband's heart. I placed my husband in Our Lord's hands.

After only two hours, the surgeon came to see me. During the procedure, he had a "gut feeling" to stop, fearing it could cause a heart attack or stroke. Reviewing the case, the doctor put Mike on two different medications. A second procedure with different modifications was advised. Mike decided to wait until after our daughter's wedding. I looked forward to her big day, but my husband's health was never far from my mind. I just kept praying and lifting my intentions up to God.

The wedding day arrived and everything went beautifully. We had arranged for our parish priest, Fr. Michael Cooney, to anoint Mike after the ceremony. At the reception, another family friend and priest, Fr. Richard Treml, came to bless the newlyweds and also anoint my husband. Mike later told me that he felt a surge of energy as Fr. Rich prayed.

A couple weeks later, when the day for Mike's procedure arrived, I accompanied him and waited for him to be prepped for surgery. I watched the screen as the nurse monitored his heartbeat. Everything seemed so normal to me, but I was no expert. I finally asked the nurse what she saw. She also saw nothing irregular.

The doctor was summoned. He too could find no irregularities, either, so he hooked Mike up to a heart monitor, coming in periodically to check on him. Finally, after Mike had been hooked up for four hours the doctor looked Mike in the eyes and said, "It's gone. You don't need surgery."

We were shocked. I asked the doctor if he believed in the power of prayer and miracles. He smiled and answered, "Yes, I do. There is no other explanation for this."

It has been a year since this miracle. I continue to pray often, but now, they are prayers of thanksgiving.

— Gloria Bishop

Gloria Bishop writes from Clinton Township, Michigan.

Sr. Faustina's Miracle

In 1995, I was given three to five years to live. My doctor declared me incurable and said I would never return to a normal life style. I am living proof that miracles do happen. Eight years after the grim prognosis, my permanent heart ailment is gone and I am as healthy as I have ever been.

I have been blessed by the Lord with a wonderful healing through Sr. Faustina's intercession. My healing became the canonization miracle. So it was awesome to stand alongside the Holy Father on April 30, 2000 and hear him declare Sr. Maria Faustina the first saint of the Great Jubilee Year. And now, more people than ever will hear of the message of mercy.

At the age of forty-eight, I was at peace learning that I could expect only a few more years of life on earth. I needed surgery to remove a calcified aortic valve and to insert an artificial valve. There was even some doubt that I could survive the surgery. And although the operation was successful, my damaged heart relegated me to "uninsurable" status—not long for this world. I recovered slowly and attempted to resume my activities as pastor of Holy Rosary parish in Baltimore, Maryland, but I tired easily and needed frequent rests.

On October 5, 1995, the feast day of St. Faustina (who was then declared "blessed"), I gathered with friends for prayer at my church. After a time of prayer for the healing of my heart through Sr. Faustina's intercession, I venerated a first class relic of hers and then collapsed. I felt paralyzed but was completely at peace.

On my subsequent visit to my cardiologist he did a physical exam and then an echocardiogram. Looking at the results he shook his head and stared at me for what seemed like an eternity. Then, he finally said, "Someone has intervened for you. I've never seen this before. Your heart is completely normal."

I know in my heart that Sr. Faustina put in a word with Jesus, and the mercy flowing from His Heart touched mine. It is as simple as that.

After almost three years of examining me and my medical records, doctors and theologians from the Congregation for the Cause of Saints concluded an exhaustive investigation of the healing. Dr. Valentin Fuster, a world-renowned cardiologist from Mount Sinai's School of Medicine, sat on the panel of doctors that reviewed my healing. He indicated that there was no known case of recovery from my condition—aortic insufficiency. And on December 20, 1999, Pope John Paul II ordered publication of the fact of the healing as a miracle through Sr. Faustina's intercession, leading to her canonization on Mercy Sunday, April 30, in St. Peter's Square.

As a result of this miracle, people have come in droves to the Baltimore shrine. The number of people visiting Holy Rosary Church for daily Mass has also increased. On the second Sunday of every month, our parish holds Divine Mercy devotions. We usually have more than fifty people stay after Mass to receive the Anointing of the Sick and venerate St. Faustina's relic. There's a real hunger for the Lord's healing touch in people's lives.

People sometimes ask, "Why you?" I even ask that question. My guess is that Sr. Faustina had a devotion to the priesthood because the mercy of God flows through priests in the sacraments of Reconciliation and the

Eucharist. From the heart of Jesus flows God's mercy, and it was my healed heart that finalized Sr. Faustina's canonization. Perhaps she got a little ethnic. She was a Polish nun and I am a Polish American. But whatever the reason, as a priest I am in a good position to proclaim this message. And that I will do for however many days I have left on this earth.

— Fr. Ronald P. Pytel

Fr. Ronald Pytel has been pastor of Holy Rosary Parish in East Baltimore since 1991.

The Greater the Sinner, the Greater the Mercy

I watched as many poor people walked about in tattered clothing, visiting, eating tacos ... and smiling. "What do they have to be so happy about?" I wondered. I was attending a medical conference in Mexico City in 1991 and had taken time out to visit the Shrine of Our Lady of Guadalupe. The image of our Blessed Mother on the five-hundred-year-old cactus fibers of a peasant's tilma is truly amazing. But it was the crowd milling around outside the shrine that captured my attention. I could not understand why I, a successful physician with a prestigious medical practice in Florida, should find happiness so elusive while joy radiated off these poor peasants?

I had it all, and yet I had nothing. In spite of money, status, material possessions, and a beautiful family, personal satisfaction eluded me. The fact that I had a wonderful wife and three children and was a Catholic since birth should have been my compass in life. Instead, I was on a course for disaster. Trapped in a lifestyle of women, materialism, and workaholic tendencies, I was sinking fast. There's a saying: "Your sin will find you out," and thankfully, mine did. Although I did not feel that way at the time, by being confronted with my involvement with other women, the last shreds of my life began to unravel. Looking back, I can see I was not thinking straight. My twisted life needed to unravel before I could begin again to be straight with my family and with God.

When I hit rock bottom, I was anxious and depressed, wondering how I ever could rebuild my life with who I was. How could my wife, Susan, and I start to build a new relationship on the rubble of my past? It was at this time that a friend sent me literature on the devotion of Divine Mercy. The pamphlet explained that the Polish nun, Saint Faustina, canonized in 2000 and the first saint of the new millennium, had written a diary in which she recorded her mystical experiences—in particular Jesus Christ's desire that the world accept His unfathomable mercy. When I read, "The greater the sinner, the greater the right he has to my Mercy (*Diary of St. Faustina*, 723)," I was overcome with remorse and gratitude. Tears of sorrow flowed like a river, as if expelling the pus of my wounds of sin. I read the words again and again realizing that in the depths of sin, there was help—even for me.

Christ's Divine Mercy became a life jacket that kept me afloat and kept me from drowning in a sea of misery. Later that year, in 1992, Susan and I went to counseling and slowly, through God's grace, began constructing a solid marriage. We both became part of the Divine Mercy ministry, sharing our own story, as well as educating people on Divine Mercy and the true presence of Jesus in the Eucharist.

Initially, I balanced my medical practice with volunteering in the ministry, but over the ensuing five years, I felt called to leave medicine behind. I cried the day I wrote a letter to the medical board giving up my license to practice medicine. But in my heart, I fully believed God was calling me out of one healing ministry to another; from the physical to the spiritual. Although it meant making big changes in our lifestyle, Susan and I decided we could manage by living off our savings. It was a new path in our walk down the road of life. I knew we needed to fully trust in God.

On September 9, 1995, the fruit of our healed marriage was born—John Paul. He was special from the start. At his birth, he struggled with life; turning blue and unable to breathe. We prayed intently and John Paul soon stabilized and fully rebounded. A friend distributing Holy Communion walked into the room and said, "Wow, what happened? I can really feel the presence of God."

I understood in my heart how God had truly blessed us. My three oldest, Andrea, thirteen, Bryan eleven, and Patricia, eight, did not always fully understand the changes of going from being doctor's kids to children of one dedicated to simple life of service to God. And yet they surely benefited from the renewal of our marriage and my commitment to fatherhood as a holy vocation.

In early November, fourteen months later, I returned home from a conference in the early morning hours. That evening a Mass was going to be celebrated in our home. In spite of very little sleep, I awoke early to take care of some of the outside work. I stepped onto our back patio, opened the gate to our swimming pool, and walked out to the backyard. Young Bryan suddenly yelled from the front for help starting the lawnmower. After helping him, I was reminded that it was time to drive Andrea to swim practice. We jumped in the car with Patricia and hurried off.

While on our way, I received a call on my cell phone from Bryan. "Dad," he said in a strained voice, "John Paul is dead. Someone left the pool gate open."

Susan had found John Paul lifeless; he was not breathing and did not have a palpable heart beat. As a trained nurse, she was already administering CPR in an effort to pump life back into John Paul's little fourteen-month-old body.

I told the girls what had happened and we immediately said a Hail Mary together. The rest of the drive was spent in tears and silent prayers. "Jesus, have mercy on

John Paul and me," I cried. Guilt overwhelmed me as I envisioned my helpless little boy bobbing up and down in the pool, all because I left the gate open. John Paul had been a part of my healing—a child of promise for Susan and me. "Jesus, why would You take him from us now?," my heart cried.

Then, as I frantically had to wait at a red light, I was suddenly hit with the scripture story from Genesis of Abraham being asked to offer his son, Isaac, up to God. "God, are you asking me for my son?" I asked, my heart breaking. It was the moment of truth for me. I had been preaching trust in God's Divine Mercy for four years. God was calling me to a deeper trust. I wanted my little boy to live. I loved him with all my heart. Could I accept God's will if it meant never holding John Paul again in this life?

"Jesus," I prayed. "I trust in You, in all situations. I submit to Your will, whatever that means." I told God that I did not understand why He would take John Paul from us at this time, but that I offered my son back to Him. I also thanked God for the time He had given us with John Paul. I told Jesus that I placed my trust in Him and wanted only that His will be done. I reflected on the deep trust of Abraham as he was told to sacrifice Isaac. I felt a deep sense of peace after that.

When we arrived at the house, the emergency squad had also just gotten there. Although John Paul was bloated and unresponsive, Susan felt a slight pulse after doing CPR. I was ecstatic. There was still hope! Upon arriving at the hospital, I called my sister who lives in another town and asked her to pray for John Paul that night with her prayer group. Over the next thirty-six hours, John Paul's mental clarity improved hourly. Within two days, he was released, totally normal!

I saw my sister a couple of weeks later as she drove up to join our family for Thanksgiving. She said to me, "I never told you this story. But the morning following our prayer group, my friend, Irma, called and said that she knew John Paul was going to recover. While praying in the morning, she had a vision of Abraham offering Isaac back to God the Father. Then Jesus, The Divine Mercy, stepped in the middle and gave him back." Tears streamed down my cheeks, and I said to her, "Well, let me tell you the rest of the story ... ."

I'm happy to report that John Paul, our child of the promise, is now a typical, healthy seven-year-old boy. And the rest of the story is really that I have never been the same since that lesson in trusting Jesus. In fact, "Divine Mercy as a Way of Life" sums up the mission of Eucharistic Apostles of The Divine Mercy (EADM), the lay outreach ministry that I founded in 1996—the same year that I almost lost my son.

— Bryan S. Thatcher, MD

Dr. Bryan S. Thatcher and his wife, Susan, now have two more children, Christopher Michael, five, and Elizabeth Rose, three. Bryan is the founder and director of Eucharistic Apostles of the Divine Mercy. This ministry, which is now active in sixteen countries, is dedicated to serving the poor, spreading the message of Divine Mercy, and educating people on the true presence of Jesus Christ in the Eucharist. Visit www.thedivinemercy.org for more information.

See pictures for this story at www.AmazingGraceOnLine.net/Heart

Chapter 6

Life is Precious

Francisco the Shoeless

I stopped and watched a familiar Guatemalan beggar boy as he carefully searched through the garbage-filled gutter that ran along the outside of my home. I knew he had to be scrounging for food so I called out to get his attention. For a second I thought he might have glanced up at me, but then I realized I just happened to be standing where he looked. I felt the same disappointment I had felt with him many times before. Even though he was filthy, shoeless, dressed in rags, and obviously hungry, my shouted offers of help were repeatedly ignored.

"Why," I wondered, "doesn't he want my help?"

As the founder and director of The God's Child Project, it is my job to feed, clothe, and educate the poorest of the poor. During my twenty-plus years as a Catholic missionary, I have seen hundreds of thousands of poor children and homeless families. But this particular boy puzzled me. It was obvious he needed help, yet he seemingly would have none of it.

Leaving him alone, I walked back to the orphanage and began to pore over the financial books. Frustrated at the realization that we were going to end the fiscal year two thousand dollars in debt, I had to make a difficult decision.

"We will not accept any more children into the program this year," I told our staff and volunteers in a strong, clear voice. "We simply can't do it. How can we take in any more children when we can't even feed those we already have?"

Even though I hated the thought of turning needy children away, this time I was determined to stick by my decision.

Two days later, a surprise visitor knocked at my door. It was my shoeless friend! Covered with lice and foul smelling, he held up his hand and made a strange guttural sound from his throat. At first I was confused, but then it hit me that he was deaf and could not speak. The poor child had ignored me all that time because he had never heard me call to him.

My confused smile broke into very loud laughter. God had sent me the one boy in all of Guatemala who could get me to break my commitment not to accept another child. God was letting me know it was He and not I who was ultimately in charge of such things.

Francisco joined our mission that very same day. Abandoned by his father at birth, he was raised in the streets by an indifferent, alcoholic mother. When he was six-months old, a severe illness robbed him of his hearing. He had been begging on the streets for food since the age of four. The streets became his home. His bed was wherever he laid down to sleep at night.

Francisco came into our very large family that day bringing with him bad habits, lice, fleas and rotted teeth. He also came with a very sharp mind, survival instincts, and keen emotions. Violence on TV could bring forth an anguished cry just as quickly as watching a mother kiss her son good night would bring tears to his eyes. I can only guess at the nightmares that often disrupted his sleep.

Over the years, Francisco was taught to communicate and he was able to receive an education. When his grade-school education came to an end at the mainstream public school, the teachers pooled their examination scores to determine the valedictorian. On the day of grade school graduation, it was Francisco who was asked to come up and receive the honor—much to his surprise, but not to that of his wildly cheering classmates.

In times of desperation and when the hard work seems too much, I am sometimes tempted to give up. It is at those times, however, that I think of Francisco. He is on his own now, working full-time and still studying on weekends. Because of his physical limitations, his salary is low. Still, he smiles a lot and works hard. He visits his mother who abandoned him to the streets so many years ago, and he goes to Mass often. I regularly ask our Blessed Mother to watch over this special child of God. I believe that she already has.

— Patrick Atkinson

As a Catholic missionary for the last twenty years, Patrick J. Atkinson founded and served as the executive director of seventy-two different schools, clinics, legal advocacy centers, and residences for poor children and homeless families in the United States, Central America, Southeast Asia, and Africa. In addition to serving the poor, Patrick is a nationally-known speaker and award-winning photographer and writer. To learn more about his current effort, The God's Child project, visit www.GodsChild.org.

True Champion

Can you imagine standing by your husband's side while fifteen hundred people attend an event in his honor to demonstrate their respect for him? "A true champion" is what many called my husband, Joe. When he was a starting fullback at North Dakota State University, his former coach said he always did his job and did whatever he needed to do to win. Later, as a head football coach and social studies teacher, Joe inspired kids to do the same.

After Joe successfully taught and coached at Devil's Lake High School for several years, the people of Devil's Lake named their football field after him. At the dedication of Joe Roller Field, people from his past and present, some traveling great distances, came to tell Joe about the impact he had on their lives. It could have been a scene out of a melodramatic movie. But this was not a fictional movie; it was real. And Joe's life now was not so wonderful; he was dying of Lou Gehrig's disease—technically known as amyotrophic lateral sclerosis (ALS).

Joe came home one cold evening after helping a friend erect a grain bin. He had been unable to grip a hammer. As a physical therapist, I knew it could be serious. After eliminating several neurological conditions, his doctor determined it was ALS. We were devastated. We knew it was incurable and ultimately fatal. Although the neurologist gave us a glimmer of hope when he said it was possible the symptoms could stop with the right arm and never progress, within weeks the symptoms spread. Joe was given three to five years to live. We told our two children, Matthew, eleven and Rebecca, nine, right away.

Everyone cried and then we did the only thing we could: carry on with our lives.

It was 1986 and we had been married for thirteen happy years. Now, suddenly our lives had a stop watch over them—each precious moment ticking away. More than anything, I wanted to keep joy in our home. Partly because of this goal but mostly because of Joe's resiliency, the joy was there, despite our fear and Joe's gradual loss of physical function. Joe taught high school for another three years before his increasing physical disability made it impossible.

For advocates of euthanasia or assisted suicide, that might have been the point at which they would opt to check out of this world. End it before the person loses his dignity, right? Wrong. Joe lived a full eight years after his diagnosis—and full they were, not just for him but for those around him.

Our Matthew, a 6-foot-1, 188-pound senior football star, often ran home to feed his dad and take him to the bathroom. If Rebecca or Matthew needed a lecture on behavior, it may have taken their Dad half an hour to deliver it due to his difficulty speaking, but they patiently listened and showed respect. In a newspaper article written about the beauty of Matthew's relationship with his father, Matthew was quoted as saying: "It's just respect ... it's not that difficult." He said the time spent caring for his dad was minimal compared to the time they spent talking.

Joe's physical abilities proceeded to fade, but his presence grew larger. We took him everywhere with us: Mass on Sunday, basketball and football games, and community gatherings. Hundreds of people interacted with him and our family through his declining years. People showed their love and compassion in so many ways. Sometimes people who wished to remain anonymous sent money and cards. It was through this ordeal that I came to truly understand that a person's suffering and disability are things from which we can all grow. Reaching out in love and charity, when multiplied by hundreds of people, results in a better society where people love and care for one another. If Joe had skipped those years, hundreds of people would have missed the opportunity to give and to admire Joe's fortitude and the fact that he could still smile.

Matthew, now married and the father of one, is doing his residency in neurology. To help with expenses during medical school, he worked with a quadriplegic. This speaks volumes about the person he has become. Rebecca is close to becoming a dentist. She too played an essential part in keeping our family whole and working, right up until the end. It was a lot for two teenagers to process, but they ultimately grew through the experience.

Two days before he died, Joe told me how to fix the TV remote control. The day before he died I was busy with my usual Saturday routine when I happened to catch Joe's beautiful blue eyes looking at me with total love and peace. That look was burned into my memory and sustained me through my grief. On Palm Sunday, Joe began struggling for air. I called an ambulance. Although I had spent eight years knowing that moment would come, I was not ready for it.

I still miss Joe, but I am thankful I did not miss a minute of those last eight years. A few months after his death, I was troubled by occasional shortness of breath. "Is there something wrong with my lungs?" I wondered one night in bed, unable to sleep. My leg inadvertently hit the TV remote control—the one Joe helped me fix just before he died. An infomercial came on explaining the most common symptom of anxiety—shortness of breath.

"Of course," I thought. "That's what I'm experiencing." I thanked Joe for the explanation. I had not just taken care of Joe, he had also cared for me right up until the end. I believe he still does.

— Jodi Roller

Jodi Roller is an associate professor and director of the Physical Therapy Program at the University of Mary. She recently completed her doctorate in Educational Leadership from the University of St. Thomas in Minneapolis. She resides in Bismarck, North Dakota.

The Smallest Stone

After the results of my ultrasound, Dr. Christopher sat down in a chair across from my husband, Craig, and me. Her expression looked grim. Craig and I gripped each others' hands even more tightly. "Your baby has anencephaly."

"There is a plate of cells called the neural plate that rolls up to form the neural tube, which becomes the spine and brain," the doctor explained. "For some reason your baby's tube did not seal properly, so only the most primitive brain stem was able to develop."

I pressed my knees together to stop them from shaking. I pictured a child with a gaping hole in its head. "What kind of a life will it have?"

"These babies have just enough of a brain stem to go full-term, but they rarely survive the birthing process," Dr. Christopher explained. "If they are born alive, they usually live for only an hour or so." Her eyes filled with tears. "I'm so sorry," she said, pressing her hand on ours.

This was the last thing I had expected. I looked at Craig's face. For once I was utterly at a loss for words. "If you wish, you may terminate the pregnancy now," she said in her kindest tone. "I'll leave you two alone to discuss it."

As soon as the door closed, Craig began to cry, something I had not seen him do since the joyful tears of our wedding day. "I'd have rather had a disabled child," he whispered.

"Me too," I said through my tears. I put my hand on my slightly rounded stomach, wanting to hold my baby

close while I still could. "I cannot end this baby's life," I
said.

"Neither can I," Craig agreed.

✍

"Push! You can do it!   Here comes the head!"   Dr.
Christopher cried.   I tried to forget that in a moment
'hello' would mean goodbye. Please God, let my baby be
born alive, I prayed, and tried to concentrate on bearing
down. "It's a boy, and he's alive!" cried Dr. Christopher in
jubilation.

Alive! It was the moment I'd been praying for and yet
dreading for the last six months. What if I was so repulsed
by the way he looked that I could not bring myself to hold
him during his last moments with us?   She was turning
toward me, bringing him to me. I did not want to see his
head. "Wait! Put a hat ..."

"Lisa, he needs you." She put him in my arms.

The moment I held him nothing else mattered. "Oh
my darling Aaron," I murmured.   At the sound of my
voice he turned his face toward mine, and the swollen lids
parted just a little. He opened his mouth and made a tiny
sound, then closed his eyes and nestled down in his blanket. He didn't seem to be in any distress at all. The head
I had been so afraid of was small and ended just above his
eyebrows in a little topknot of skin.   I lifted the blanket.
From the eyes down he was heartbreakingly perfect.
Craig put one finger into the tiny hand.   We looked
deeply into each other's eyes and smiled. It was a quiet
sort of joy, but joy nonetheless.

We called Father Tom, even though it was after midnight, and he arrived in record time.   My mother and

brother, and Craig's sister and her husband were there. It was the only time I had ever seen my brother-in-law so subdued. He wiped his eyes when he thought no one was looking. Aaron even had godparents there; some dear friends had asked us if they could be his godparents as soon as the anencephaly had been diagnosed.

Throughout the entire baptism I felt a profound sense of serenity. It was tinged with sadness, but for one hour we celebrated the gift of our child. As soon as Father Tom pronounced the final blessing, Aaron suddenly felt different to me.

"Would you check him please?" I asked the nurse.

She placed the stethoscope on his tiny chest. "He's gone." She pressed her lips together and tears welled in her eyes.

The next morning my brother came to visit me. "Lisa, you know I'm not a religious person, but there was a holy feeling in that room last night."

"I felt it too."

"You know what's really weird? After I left the hospital last night I went home and actually opened my Bible. I don't think I've touched it since Dad left Mom. I read exactly what I needed to 'hear', and started to bawl like a baby."

The funeral was lovelier than any I've been to before or since. My friends in the diocesan choir outdid themselves. It was a perfect spring day. The sweet smell of damp earth was in the air. I was able to walk away from that little casket without a tear. I knew that was not where Aaron was.

At the luncheon I made a beeline for Yasi, one of my favorite cousins. "How's Ken?" I asked.

"Funny you should ask," she laughed. "You know how I've been agonizing over whether to marry him?

Well, we had plans for today, but I was sure Ken would understand my going to the funeral, but he hit the ceiling."

"I'm so sorry," I said.

"Don't be," she said. "I don't think I ever would have been able to see him for what he was if not for Aaron. I broke up with him, and I couldn't be happier!"

The day after the funeral our neighbor Molly dropped off a loaf of freshly baked bread and a card. In the card, she wrote about a baby girl she had lost in the late fifties. She had never been allowed to see the baby. She never experienced closure until she went to Aaron's funeral. "Now," she wrote, "I am at peace with it."

A few days later my mood was especially bleak. It had been gray, cold, and rainy ever since the funeral. I was huddled on the couch when Craig came in with the mail. There was a card from Healing the Children, the organization we had encouraged people to send their donations to. They wrote that they had received enough money to fly two children from Nicaragua to the U.S. for life-saving operations. One of the children was a little girl with a cyst the size of an adult fist in her nasal passage.

I stared out the window at a puddle on the front landing. It had stopped raining. A tiny drop of water fell into into the puddle forming small ripples. It occurred to me that Aaron was like a tiny stone that had been tossed into an immense lake. Even the smallest stone creates ripples.

— Lisa Schreiner

Lisa Schreiner, her husband Craig, and their three boys are voracious readers who love to go camping together as a family. She is a part-time teacher and catechist for her parish and also teaches science enrichment once a week for the Holy Family Homeschoolers organization. She and her family live in Middletown, Wisconsin.

Grace Comes in Special Packages

Some gifts are not seen as such when they are first given. This is often true when a family first discovers that they will soon welcome a new child with a disability. Perhaps this is because of the special challenges that come with handicaps, or maybe it's because our culture places a high premium on beauty, efficiency, and comfort. I have discovered, however, that God can have wonderful things in store for us, despite our limited perspectives.

My first three children were perfectly healthy when they born. Everyone I knew had healthy babies. So it was a little unusual that I began to specifically pray during my fourth pregnancy for a healthy baby. I look back now and see that this was surely God's way of gently preparing me for our son's birth.

Andrew was born on the evening of May 4, 1995. It was an easy delivery and we were overjoyed to welcome our new son into our family. As I cuddled my newborn, the nurses asked me pointed questions such as, "Does he look like your other children?"

"Oh, yes," I replied. He appeared to be just as healthy as my other three children. The doctor gave us no reason for concern, so Dave went home that evening and I went to sleep content and full of peace.

The next morning our pediatrician came to see me. She announced, "Your baby has Down Syndrome." After giving me dire predictions of all he would not achieve in the future, she left. Distraught, I called Dave to break the news to him. He came to the hospital right away.

I feared something I had done during my pregnancy had caused Andrew to have Down Syndrome. The doctor later assured me that DS is a genetic disorder present from the moment of conception. Still, we struggled with unanswered questions. What would he grow to be like? How, we wondered, would having a disabled child affect our family?

Tears filled our first full day with Andrew. I kept rocking him and saying, "My poor baby, my poor baby." Although I cried for my little boy, my heart brimmed with love. I knew he was a blessing from God.

Filled with love and uncertainty, we brought Andrew home. Yet I was surprised at the similarities between taking care of a DS baby and our other babies. As Andrew grew, there were special challenges for our family, as expected. But the day I walked through our door with him, I really had no idea just how much he would change our family.

We have learned so much about God, the value of life, and our very own selves through the young life of Andrew. But mostly, we see God more clearly. He somehow feels closer to us since Andrew came into our lives.

One morning, I was lying on my bed with the other kids. I faintly heard some babbling coming from Andrew's room. It was so unusual to hear such long vocalizations of any kind so I brought him to my room and asked him, "Who were you talking to?" This was a rhetorical question because he did not speak at all. He had a vocabulary of perhaps five words. To my astonishment, he said, "I was praying."

Not trusting my ears, I looked at my oldest son, Chris, and asked, "Did he say what I thought he said?" Chris confirmed it: "He said 'I was praying.'" With that, Andrew piped up "to Jesus," just to eliminate any possible confusion!

Another time he recited the whole Our Father during a period in his life when three- and four-word sentences were the norm. Today, he keeps pace with the family by leading us in one decade of the rosary during our family prayers. He closes out each rosary by standing up, raising his arms, and saying, "God bless my family."

Though people may see nothing special in these instances, we do because we believe that only God could bring them about. There really is no earthly explanation. We believe they were given to us to remind us of how we are to approach God. We should approach him with a pure love and a child-like trust, knowing that He exists and believing He will care for us.

Andrew loves with a pure love. This is why so many are drawn to him. Crossing guards, teachers, and relatives see no guile or selfish motives in him. And we all receive his love with joy. How valuable a witness he is to a world that can be cunning, calculated, and cold.

The Bible says that God has kept some secrets from the "learned and wise" and given them to the "little ones." This seems to be the case with Andrew. His life is a testimony to the value of humility.

Of course, Andrew is far from perfect. He can be stubborn and frustrating. He can lose his glasses, run off on his own, flush things down the toilet (five weeks in a row), or extend the sign of peace a little longer than the rest of the congregation at Mass. But he is tangible proof that every person has a unique value, not because of what he does but because of who he is.

One of the gifts he has brought us is a greater sense of gratitude and thankfulness. Even the smallest accomplishment gives us reason to rejoice, because each milestone is so hard won. What may take a healthy child two days to accomplish might take Andrew two years. His accomplishments cause me to earnestly pray, "Thank you, God."

When Andrew was a baby, people often told me that God picked us to be his parents because we were special. That was comforting to us at the time. But now, I truly feel that God gave us Andrew precisely because we needed him more than he needed us. It is true that God does not always give you what you ask for, but what you need. We have grown in our love of life and our understanding of God's love for humanity.

A handicapped child can be an extraordinary blessing to a family if we see him as a gift. Yes, he comes with challenges, but the blessings have outweighed them one hundred to one. Andrew has helped draw us closer to God. In addition, I believe our celebration of Andrew's life has been a witness to others‹a witness that says that every life is valuable and that God has a purpose for each of our lives.

It is a sad situation when the world places value on someone based on their physical ability, some even resorting to the horror of abortion to avoid what they perceive to be a cross. Andrew and many like him who have Down Syndrome are rich blessings and, if embraced, can transform the very family whom has been entrusted with his care. Truly, life in all forms is precious.

— Teresa Santoleri

Teresa Santolieri is the mother of five children, four boys and one girl. Teresa and her husband, Dave, are very involved in the pro-life movement.

Teresa teaches chastity education to the youth of her area, and she and her family are involved with an orphanage in Honduras called Amigos de Jesus. The Santolieris enjoy reading, traveling and playing games together as a family. They reside in Glen Mills, Pennsylvania.

See pictures related to this story at www.AmazingGraceOnLine.net/Heart

The Play of the Year

Jack Porter is seventeen, but he can't read, can barely scrawl his first name and often mixes up the letters at that. So how come we're all learning something from him?

In three years on the Northwest High Football team, in McDermott, Ohio, Jake had never run with the ball. Or made a tackle. He'd barely stepped on the field. That's about right for a kid with chromosomal fragile x syndrome, a disorder that is a common cause of mental retardation.

But every day after school, Jake, who attends special-ed classes, races to team practices: football, basketball, track. He never plays, but seldom misses one.

That's why it seemed crazy when, with five seconds left in a game that Northwest was losing 42-0, Jake trotted out to the huddle. The plan was for him to get the handoff and take a knee.

Northwest's coach and Jake's best friend, Dave Frantz, called a timeout to talk about it with the opposing coach, Waverly's Derek Dewitt. Fans could see there was a disagreement. Dewitt was shaking his head and waving his arms.

After the ref stepped in, play resumed and Jake got the ball. He started to genuflect, as he'd practiced all week. Teammates stopped him and told him to run, but Jake started going in the wrong direction. The back judge rerouted him toward the line of scrimmage.

Suddenly, the Waverly defense parted like peasants for the king and urged him to go on his grinning sprint to the end zone. Imagine having twenty-one teammates on the field. In the stands mothers cried and fathers roared. Players on both sidelines held their helmets to the sky and whooped.

In the red-cheeked glee afterward, Jake's mom, Liz, a single parent and a waitress at a coffee shop, ran up to the 295-pound Dewitt to thank him. But she was so emotional, no words would come.

Turns out that before the play Dewitt had called his defense over and said, "They're going to give the ball to number 45. Do not touch him! Open up a hole and let him score! Understand?"

It's not the kind of thing you expect to come out of a football coach's mouth, but then Derek Dewitt is not your typical coach. Originally from the Los Angeles area, he is the first black coach in the fifty-seven-year history of a conference made up of schools along the Ohio-Kentucky border. He's already heard the "n-word" at two road games this season, once through the windows of a locker room. Yet he was willing to give up his first shutout for a white kid he had met only two hours earlier.

"I told Derek before the play, 'This is the young man we talked about on the phone,'" Frantz recalled. "He's just going to get the ball and take a knee." But Derek kept saying, 'No I want him to score.' I couldn't talk him out of it!"

Dewitt recalls being impressed when he met Jake. "All my players knew him from track," Dewitt said. "So, when the time came, touching the ball just didn't seem good enough." (By the way, Dewitt and his team got their shutout the next week, 7-0 against Cincinnati Mariemont.)

Into every parade a few stink bombs must fall. Mark

Madden of the *Pittsburgh Post-Gazette* grumbled that if the mentally challenged want to participate in sports, "let them do it at the Special Olympics. Leave high school football alone, and for heaven's sake, don't put the fix in." A few over-testosteroned Neanderthals on an Internet site complained, "That isn't football." No, it became bigger than football. Since it happened, people in the two towns just seem to be treating one another better. Kids in the two schools walk around beaming. "I have this bully in one of my phys-ed classes," says Dewitt. "He's a rough, out-for-himself type kid. The other day I saw him helping a couple of special-needs kids play basketball. I about fell over."

Jake is no different, though. Still happy as a frog in a bog. Still signs the teachers' register in the principal's office every morning, ready to work. Still gets sent on errands, forgets where he's going and ends up in Frantz's office. Still talks all the time only now it's to NBC, ESPN and affiliates from CBS and Fox about his touchdown that won the game.

Yeah, Jake Porter thinks his forty-nine-yard run made for a comeback victory. He thinks he was the hero. He thinks that's why there were so many grins and streaks down people's faces.

Smart kid.

— Rick Reilly

Rick Reilly is a former altar boy, but he is best known as the award-winning writer for Sports Illustrated.

I Said a Prayer for You Today

I said a prayer for you today
And know God must have heard.
I felt the answer in my heart
Although He spoke no word!

I didn't ask for wealth or fame
(I knew you wouldn't mind).
I asked Him to send treasures
Of a far more lasting kind!

I asked that He'd be near you
At the start of each new day;
To grant your health and blessings
And friends to share your way!

I asked for happiness for you
In all things great and small.
But it was for His loving care
I prayed the most of all!

— Author unknown

We Believe You!

In the late 1990's I worked in the activities department at a local nursing home, where we often brought out the Alzheimers Unit residents to join the other residents' activities. Some days Arlene, my co-worker, and I really wondered if it was worth all the effort. It took a considerable amount of vigilance just to keep them in the room, let alone involved. We could not help but question what they were getting out of it and how much they really understood of anything. But there we were one Good Friday afternoon with a resident on each arm and a wheelchair in front. We baby-stepped our way down the hall to watch a video about Our Lord's crucifixion and resurrection in the main activity room.

When Arlene and I finally succeeded in getting everyone and every wheelchair into position, we plopped down, wet with perspiration and thankful to be off our feet. As we scanned the darkened room, the residents' eyes seemed to be fixed on the TV as Franco Zeffirelli's acclaimed production *Jesus of Nazareth* began.

I was pleasantly surprised at the quiet attention being paid to the screen. Even Frank with his short attention span was brought back every so often by a sudden change in the emotional pitch of the dialogue or the musical score.

At last came the scene where Mary Magdalene comes upon the empty tomb and sees Jesus' body not there. A man (Jesus) asks Mary why she is looking for the living among the dead. Mary runs as fast as she can back to the disciples and tells Peter and the rest with breathless excitement, "He's alive! I saw Him, I tell you!" The doubt in their eyes causes Mary to pull back . "You don't believe me ... You don't believe me!"

Then, from somewhere in that you-could-hear-a-pin-drop activity room came the clear, resolute voice of Esther, from the Alzheimer's unit, "WE BELIEVE YOU ... WE BELIEVE YOU!

— Rosemary Kadrmas

Rosemary Kadrmas is the proud mother of three boys, one of who was recently ordained a diocesan priest. When Rosemary is not busy running the CCD program in her parish, you might find her and her husband hiking across the Badlands of North Dakota. She and Vern have been married thirty-eight years and live in Bowman, North Dakota.

Let the Children Come to Me

Sighing to myself, I was mentally dreading the stampede that would ensue the minute we opened the doors for my friend's garage sale one Saturday morning in 1993. The day before had been hectic. Elaine and I had both asked each other the same question. "What is it about the American tradition of garage sales that seems to bring out the worst in some people?"

That summer had been very difficult for Elaine and her husband, Marcus. He was very ill and Elaine was struggling to run his Catholic bookstore business and maintain her own job. This garage sale was not just to clear out their basement, but to come up with enough money to keep the bookstore going.

I arrived two hours early on Friday morning to help Elaine open the sale. Cars were already lined up around the block. People had even pulled into Elaine's driveway, forcing me to park two blocks away.

Despite our efforts to get an early start and keep things under control, the sale began with mass confusion. We had to keep moving people out of the way and tell them not to start rummaging until we were set up. Elaine had rented so many tables they filled the entire three-car garage and there was no space to walk around them. Several tables needed to be placed on the driveway so shoppers could move around them easily.

The minute we opened the door to move the first table, bargain hunters pushed and shoved their way in. Some shoppers practically got into fistfights over items, insisting they had spotted a particular item first. Despite the commotion, Friday was a success.

I arrived early once again on Saturday, the second and final day of the sale. Elaine's neighbor, Tracy, came to lend us a helping hand. Her two-year-old daughter, Marcy, tagged along closely. The little girl was pretty fussy all day, and being very shy, she would have nothing to do with anyone but her mother. I had tried several times in vain to interest her in some game or other when her mom was busy. It was just one of those stages children go through, so we worked around the problem all day long.

The only thing besides her mother that Marcy seemed to care about was a battered, garden-sized statue of Jesus. When she first discovered it, she was immediately captivated, jabbering on at length into the face of Jesus.

By closing time, it had begun to rain. We decided to wait until another day to dismantle the tables, so we moved them into the garage. Elaine had ordered some pizza to celebrate a successful garage sale. We were all thrilled to know that we had raised enough money to carry the store through another couple of months, when Marcus could hopefully return to work.

Before the pizza arrived, I walked back into the garage to retrieve the one thing I had purchased—the statue of Jesus. It was too precious to throw away but so battered that no one wanted it—no one, of course, except little Marcy. "Maybe with some paint, it would look nice in my patio garden," I thought.

As I reached down to pick it up, I noticed we had forgotten to close the third garage door, and the rain was pouring in. We had problems getting the automatic door up and down the last few times, since the tables were nearly jammed against it. The door's safety mechanism was broken, and if the tables impeded it in anyway it would close on top of the table, thereby damaging the table and anything left on it. Also, the door would not reverse just by pushing the button again. It had to close completely before it could be stopped and opened again.

I hit the button then watched to make sure the door closed properly. In that instant I caught a glimpse of little Marcy as she ran toward the door. Ice-cold chills ran through me as I screamed desperately: "No, Marcy. Go back!"

Instead, to my horror, Marcy froze directly under the closing door. She had not obeyed one request from me all day due to her shyness and she was not going to start doing so now. She stubbornly shook her head "no."

As the door slowly moved down toward Marcy's little body, I was in shock. The tables blocked me from getting to her and there was no time to run through the house and out the side door to snatch her from beneath the closing garage door. In anguish I cried out: "Jesus, help me!" and my knees completely gave out as I shook from shear terror and helplessness.

As my knees hit the concrete in an almost prayer-like position, I saw the most amazing answer to my prayer. Marcy was running towards me. She was so little that she sprinted underneath the tables in a flash. She ran towards me with her arms out as though she would run into my embrace. I was crying and shaking so hard I again could only utter, "Jesus, Jesus, praise you Jesus!"

As I cried out my praise and wonder, Marcy ran right by me to hug the statue of Jesus. She ran into Jesus arms. Jesus had saved her.

— Christine Trollinger

Christine Trollinger is the author of several of the stories in this book. Her biography appears after The Badge of Grace *in Chapter One.*

One Dozen Blessings

Most families would agree that one of life's most significant events is the addition of a child to the family. For Bob
and Shari Wild, college sweethearts who married in 1967,
that was certainly the case—twelve times over. While the
Wilds had talked about having perhaps five or six children, having a dozen was something they had never
dreamed of. Nor could they have imagined what would
happen along the way.

The Wilds' first child, Karen, was born in 1968.
When their second child, Bobby, was born two years later,
their lives were turned upside down. "When he was one
day old he needed surgery for a constrictor in the small
intestine," says Shari, a petite, youthful-looking fifty-four.
"We had him baptized because the doctors gave him only
a fifty percent chance of survival."

The couple prayed as the surgery progressed into the
night.

"Here he was, maybe not going to live, but God did
something very special for me," says Shari. "I felt I heard
God speak to my heart that Bobby belonged to Him, not
to me. I knew that all I could do was to pray that God's
will would be done." For Shari it was the major event that
most affected her faith life. "Right after that the homilies
and the Gospel readings at Mass just seemed to come
more alive for me than they had in the past," she says. "It
made me eager to find a deeper relationship with the
Lord. I had a very strong desire to serve God more, to
show Him how thankful I was."

Bobby survived the surgery, but was not out of the woods. He failed to thrive and, at two months, was diagnosed with cystic fibrosis. Bob and Shari were devastated when they were told he would most likely not survive beyond the age of five or six and that they were both carriers of the disease.

In the early seventies the family moved to Ann Arbor and became involved in a prayer group. "It was just what we needed then," says Shari. "We learned how to let the Holy Spirit into our lives." Shortly after the group began praying for Bobby, who was two at the time, doctors at University of Michigan thought he had been misdiagnosed. Further testing revealed he still had CF but appeared very healthy. His pediatrician decided to remove him from prophylactic antibiotics, which most CF patients need to prevent lung infections. He has never had to go back on them.

Bobby is now thirty-one, married, and an engineer at Ford Motor Co. "The doctors have told him there is no reason he can't live a normal life span," says Shari. "We just know that it is God's blessing."

And the blessings continued.

Knowing they had a significant chance of having another child with cystic fibrosis, the Wilds began to consider adoption. "We wanted more children. We were seeking spiritual direction," said Bob, fifty-six, an engineer for General Motors. "It was on a men's retreat that I said, 'Look, Lord, one of the things I want to get out of this retreat is whether or not we should adopt.'"

Bob felt directed to a Bible passage that made it clear to him they should do just that. Within days the Wilds were at the Washtenaw Department of Social Services leafing through a book with a different child pictured on each page. "It was like a multi-list of kids with disabilities of one sort or another," Bob recalls. When the couple explained their reason for adopting, the caseworker showed them a photo of a five-year-old little boy, right between the ages of Karen and Bobby. The little face that smiled back at them from the album page looked incredibly like their own son. It belonged to Rick, a child who had been in need of a home for two years. He too had cystic fibrosis.

Within weeks, Rick was theirs. "It was so exciting," says Shari. "I could hardly believe it, it happened so fast." It turned out that Rick's pediatrician was the same one that Bobby had had as an infant. She was able to inform the Wilds that Rick had a more severe case of the disease than Bobby did and they shouldn't expect him to live beyond fifteen. But Rick lived to the age of thirty, dying just two years ago. As he grew older and lived on his own, Rick began to drift away from the Church. During his last days he was hospitalized, and Shari went to be by his side. "As I was driving to the hospital," Shari remembers, "I was praying for him and I felt the Lord was saying, 'Don't worry, I've taken care of everything.'"

Rick was in a semi-comatose state. But the day before he died, Shari remembers, "He came out of the coma for about a half hour and began repeating over and over, 'I love Jesus with my whole soul, my whole heart, my whole mind and my whole strength.' As he was saying this, a priest walked into the room."

Shari asked the priest to administer last rites to her son, which he did, along with general absolution. "It was probably the most special time in our lives," says Shari, in a voice choked with emotion. "Bob and I just cried and cried. I asked the priest if someone had sent him to us and he said, no, he just happened to wander into the room."

"Rick stayed awake a few more minutes. Two of his friends were visiting who also had CF, and Rick started telling them, 'You need to give your life to God.' He was kind of evangelizing them. Then he slipped back into the coma."

"I spent the night with Rick and he woke up once and looked at me and asked, 'Mom, am I going to heaven?' and I told him, 'You are, Rick, because you did all the right things.' Then he went back to sleep. Rick died the next night while we were in the room. It was the Vigil of the Ascension of Our Lord. I was holding his hand when he died. It was just as God had said—that He would take care of everything."

Undaunted by the task of having a second child with cystic fibrosis, the Wilds learned of their next child in the courtroom parking lot after the finalization of Rick's adoption. Their caseworker told them about Jennifer, a five-month-old infant who had multiple medical problems and had already endured two major surgeries. Nine days later, Jennifer joined the family.

Now twenty-six, Jennifer has been hospitalized some fifty times and has undergone forty major, minor or exploratory surgeries. Just a few months ago the Wilds learned that Jennifer's birth father had told her she was the product of a botched first-trimester abortion attempt. When Shari asked her how she had felt when hearing the information, Jennifer said, "I thought God must have a wonderful plan for my life since He allowed me to survive the abortion."

Indeed, her life had already been a series of miraculous events starting with her very survival. A missionary family staying with the Wilds prayed over Jennifer when she was a young child. Two weeks later one of her kidneys that had been pea-sized and nonfunctioning had grown to proper size and was functioning at one-hundred percent. Doctors had no explanation.

When Jennifer was nine, doctors were considering surgery to correct her spinal problems. After a priest, who had the gift of healing, said prayers over her, orthopedic specialists were amazed when X-rays revealed the spine had straightened and surgery was no longer needed. When Jennifer was about four, Shari had a feeling that God wanted her to teach her young daughter how to offer her sufferings for various intentions. Jennifer began doing that and, Shari added, continues to this day.

"One answered prayer that we know of happened when Jennifer was about nine," Shari says. "She was in the hospital and the pain would not subside. A fifty-eight-year-old woman came into our room and started talking with us. This was the children's ward, so why she was even there I don't know."

The woman, a diabetic, said a cat had clawed her and gangrene had set in. Her finger was to be amputated the next morning. Jennifer offered her suffering, and she and Shari prayed for her. The next day the woman came rushing into their room. "When they took the bandage off, her finger was perfectly normal," Shari recalls. "Amputation was not necessary."

Jennifer continues to suffer health problems. But she married three years ago and now lives in Colorado with her husband, Stan, and their adopted son, Jakob, who also had multiple health problems—a preemie of only 1 lb., 13 oz. with a cleft palate that has since been repaired.

When Jennifer was three, the Wilds traveled to Bogotá, Colombia, to bring home three-month-old Tony. Then they wanted another dark-skinned child and found it nearly impossible to adopt one in the United States. Bethany Christian Homes in Grand Rapids contacted them with the news that they were planning to travel to one of Mother Teresa's Missionaries of Charity orphanages in Bangladesh and would bring a child back for them.

Age four at the time, Raju was eager to join his new family, but political problems delayed his and other children's departure for more than a year. During that time Bob and Shari prayed and fasted until they learned that Raju, whose name they changed to Roger, was coming home. Roger could speak only Bengali, but was an eager learner. Within three months, he had learned enough English to tell his parents about his best friend who remained in Bangladesh. "Milon-airplane-you-Mommy, Daddy," Roger said to express his desire that Shari and Bob adopt his buddy. With the help of the nun who had escorted Roger and the other children to the U.S., a few political strings were pulled and Milon was soon Roger's brother. Between the two friends' adoptions, Bethany Christian Homes called the Wilds in April 1984 with a special request: Would they take in a little Korean boy who had just arrived in Chicago and had been diagnosed with terminal cancer?

"They needed a home for him to die in," Shari recalls. Jeffrey was just five-and-a-half and spoke only Korean when he came to live with them. The Wilds took their new son to U-M Hospital, where Jeffrey underwent further testing that confirmed he had a rare form of cancer—neuroepithelioma. He was given about a month to live.

"We went home and two of my friends came over and we knelt down and prayed, asking for guidance," Shari recalls. That day a call came from U-M. A doctor there said he had a friend doing research on that type of cancer at the National Institutes of Health. Arrangements had already been made for Shari and Jeffrey to fly there immediately.

Dr. Miser, whom Shari described as a Spirit-filled devout Christian with two adopted children of his own, later said to her, "God told me this one is going to make it" as soon as he saw Shari and Jeffrey come through the door. After Jeffrey's first round of chemotherapy, NIH paid for him and Shari to fly back to Michigan so he would have a chance to know his brothers and sisters.

The healing priest who had prayed over Jennifer was in town, so Bob stood in proxy for his new son at the Mass. During the Eucharistic prayers, the priest announced that he felt the Holy Spirit wanted to work with, among other conditions, tumorous cancers, and that tumors would just melt away in the next few weeks.

By the end of Jeffrey's three-week stay at home, a tumor the size of half an orange that had been on the side of his right knee was no longer visible. But the treatment at NIH was to continue. Following six rounds of chemo, radiation five days a week for five weeks was scheduled. Shari was told that Jeffrey would receive radiation so intense that his bones would no longer grow. His knee and a tumor in his pelvic region were targeted.

"The day I was to take him in for radiation," Shari remembers, "I asked the Lord to send the angels to shield those areas so that it would not affect his bone growth." She told no one of her prayer. "On the seventh day I took him in for his blood test—each day he had to have a blood test to check his white cell count," says Shari. A woman, bringing in a friend in a wheelchair, walked up to Shari and asked what she thought of NIH. "I told her I thought it was wonderful, not only for medical treatment, but also for kindness," Shari says.

The woman answered with "Praise the Lord!" They both remarked on their shared Christianity and the woman told Shari a startling story. "I'll tell you why I came over here," the woman said. "I had a dream last night. When I saw your little boy, I realized he was the one in my dream. You're going to think this is really strange, but in my dream his body was filled with little angels protecting him."

"I never saw that woman again," says Shari, still awestruck by the encounter. "After all this, you just know that God is doing all these things." Jeffrey not only lived, he grew. Now twenty-one, Jeffrey lives in Ypsilanti and walks with only a slight limp. Bob describes him as a real entrepreneur: "He owns his own business and is doing very well."

In 1988 the Wilds adopted Sandra, six, her brother Eddie, three, and sister Cherrie, twenty months. Then, one day in 1990, the kids came home from school saying there was a ten-year-old girl in foster care who lived just a mile away. They asked if the Wilds could adopt her. Anna came to live with them and is now, at twenty-one, happily reunited with her birth family. She still maintains a relationship with the Wilds.

These days life has quieted down for the Wilds, except at weddings and holidays, when most of the children, spouses and eight grandchildren get together. There are only two children at home now—Ed, age sixteen, and Cherrie, fourteen.

As they look back over the years, the Wilds remain in awe at how God's amazing grace has worked in their lives. They feel He has rewarded them many times over for their faith in Him.

— Diane Morey Hanson

You'll find Diane Morey Hanson's biography after the story Through the Wounds of Christ *in Chapter Five.*

Mom's Last First Look

When my father died one hot July evening from the toxic effects of spraying an insecticide, he left my mother a widow with seven children.

My mother was a gentle yet firm woman. God and church ruled her life, while love and the right dose of discipline guided her motherhood. The four oldest kids helped support our family financially, and together we did more than just get along. My childhood was full of rich Catholic values, security, and love.

When I was a teenager, Mom was diagnosed with cancer. She underwent a mastectomy and radiation. But rather than cure, these only brought more suffering. We did our best to keep Mom comfortable during the year-and-a-half after her diagnosis. It was the 1940's, a time when pain killers were not widely used. All Mom had to soften her cross was her ever-present rosary and the crucifix that hung in her room. Yet, somehow she always found a way to smile and ask us all, "How was your day?"

When it was clear the end was near, Mom received the last rites and we all gathered around her. Our hearts overflowed with love and sadness; it would not be long now. Suddenly, Mom lifted her head and opened her eyes wide. She looked ahead of her in awe, seeing something truly amazing and wonderful. Then, very peacefully, she lay her head back down and slipped away.

The days and weeks that followed melded into a blur of grief. But as the months turned into years, it was my mother's last moment in this world that gave me peace. She had seen something. Mom was not alone when she left us. Someone had come for her and God had given us the grace of sharing Mom's first glimpse of the eternal.

— Julie Maguire

Julie Maguire grew up one of seven children in Detroit, Michigan. This cradle Catholic is now mother to six of her own wonderful children. She and her husband have enjoyed forty-eight years of marriage and delightfully celebrated a large family reunion together last year.

Breakfast with a Champion

Every year in Washington, DC, political and religious leaders from across the United States come together for the National Prayer Breakfast. In 1994, President Bill Clinton, First Lady Hillary Clinton, and Vice President Al Gore were on hand, sitting at the distinguished head table, in anticipation of honoring a diminutive nun from a far away place well-known for her works of mercy to the poorest of the poor.

In a city that loves a good debate, this annual event is intentionally non-partisan. Speakers seem to make concerted efforts to avoid controversy. The event is attended by people of all faiths. At this particular breakfast, however, the message was anything but meek, and the speaker's talk was followed by a prolonged standing ovation from all except the President and his entourage.

Mother Teresa of Calcutta, noted humanitarian and 1971 winner of the Nobel Peace Prize, spoke of how precious life is and what we can learn from the poor. She unequivocally told those present that it is imperative for all people to stand up for life. Her words possess a power that pierced the hearts of those who heard them in 1994, and they continue to resonate the truth to all who would listen.

Here is a slightly condensed version of her speech:

∽

On the last day, Jesus will say to those at his right hand, "Come, enter the Kingdom. For I was hungry and you gave me food, I was thirsty and you gave me drink, I was sick and you visited me."

Then Jesus will turn to those on his left hand and say, "Depart from me because I was hungry and you did not feed me, I was thirsty and you did not give me drink, I was sick and you did not visit me."

These will ask him, "When did we see you hungry, or thirsty, or sick, and did not come to your help?"

And Jesus will answer them, "Whatever you neglected to do unto one of the least of these, you neglected to do unto me!"

Let us thank God for the opportunity he has given us today to have come here to pray together. We have come here especially to pray for peace, joy, and love. We are reminded that Jesus came to bring the good news to the poor. He had told us what that good news is when he said, "My peace I leave with you, my peace I give unto you." He came not to give the peace of the world, which is only that we don't bother each other. He came to give peace of heart which comes from loving, from doing good to others.

And God loved the world so much that he gave his son. God gave his son to the Virgin Mary, and what did she do with him? As soon as Jesus came into Mary's life, immediately she went in haste to give that good news. And as she came into the house of her cousin, Elizabeth, Scripture tells us that the unborn child—the child in the womb of Elizabeth—leapt with joy. While still in the womb of Mary, Jesus brought peace to John the Baptist, who leapt for joy in the womb of Elizabeth.

And as if that were not enough—as if it were not enough that God the Son should become one of us and bring peace and joy while still in the womb—Jesus also died on the Cross to show that greater love. He died for you and for me, and for that leper and for that man dying of hunger and that naked person lying in the street—not only of Calcutta, but of Africa, of everywhere. Our Sisters serve these poor people in 105 countries throughout the world. Jesus insisted that we love one another as he loves each one of us. Jesus gave his life to love us, and he tells us that he loves each one of us. And in the Gospel Jesus says very clearly, "Love as I have loved you."

Jesus died on the Cross because that is what it took for him to do good for us—to save us from our selfishness and sin. He gave up everything to do the Father's will, to show us that we too must be willing to give everything to do God's will, to love one another as he loves each of us.

St. John says that you are a liar if you say you love God and you don't love your neighbor. How can you love God whom you do not see, if you do not love your neighbor whom you see, whom you touch, with whom you live?

Jesus makes himself the hungry one, the naked one, the homeless one, the unwanted one, and he says, "You did it to me."

I can never forget the experience I had in visiting a home where they kept all these old parents of sons and daughters who had just put them into an institution and, maybe, forgotten them. I saw that in that home these old people had everything: good food, comfortable place, television, everything. But everyone was looking toward the door. And I did not see a single one with a smile on his face.

I turned to Sister and I asked, "Why do these people, who have every comfort here—why are they all looking toward the door? Why are they not smiling?" (I am so used to seeing the smiles on our people. Even the dying ones smile.) And Sister said, "This is the way it is, nearly everyday. They are expecting—they are hoping—that a son or daughter will come to visit them.

See, this neglect to love brings spiritual poverty. Maybe in our family we have somebody who is feeling lonely, who is feeling sick, who is feeling worried. Are we willing to give until it hurts, in order to be with our families? Or do we put our own interests first?

I was surprised in the West to see so many young boys and girls given to drugs. And I tried to find out why. Why is it like that, when those in the West have so many more things than those in the East? And the answer was, "Because there is no one in the family to receive them." Our children depend on us for everything: their health, their nutrition, their security, their coming to know and love God. For all of this, they look to us with trust, hope, and expectation. But often father and mother are so busy that they have no time for their children, or perhaps they are not even married, or have given up on their marriage. So the children go to the streets, and get involved in drugs, or other things. We are talking of love of the child, which is where love and peace must begin.

But I feel that the greatest destroyer of peace today is abortion, because it is a war against the child—a direct killing of the innocent child—murder by the mother herself. And if we accept that a mother can kill even her own child, how can we tell other people not to kill one another? How do we persuade a woman not to have an abortion? As always, we must persuade her with love. The father of that child, whoever he is, must also give until it hurts. By abortion, the mother does not learn to love but kills even her own child to solve her problems. And by abortion, the father is told that he does not have to take any responsibility at all for the child he has brought into the world. Any country that accepts abortion is not teaching the people to love, but to use any violence to get what they want. That is why the greatest destroyer of love and peace is abortion.

And for this I appeal in India and I appeal everywhere: "Let us bring the child back." The child is God's gift to the family. Each child is created in the special image and likeness of God for greater things—to love and to be loved. This is the only way that our world can survive, because our children are the only hope for the future. As other people are called to God, only their children can take their places.

But what does God say to us? He says, "Even if a mother could forget her child, I will not forget you. I have carved you in the palm of my hand." We are carved in the palm of his hand; that unborn child has been carved in the hand of God from conception, and is called by God to love and to be loved, not only now in this life, out forever. God can never forget us.

From our children's home in Calcutta alone, we have saved over 3,000 children from abortion. These children have brought such love and joy to their adopting parents, and have grown up so full of love and joy! I know that couples have to plan their family, and for that there is natural family planning. The way to plan the family is natural family planning, not contraception. In destroying the power of giving life, through contraception, a husband or wife is doing something to self. This turns the attention to self, and so it destroys the gift of love in him or her. In loving, the husband and wife must turn the attention to each other, as happens in natural family planning, and not to self, as happens in contraception. Once that living love is destroyed by contraception, abortion follows very easily.

The poor are very great people. They can teach us so many beautiful things. Once one of them came to thank us for teaching them natural family planning, and said: "You people who have practiced chastity, you are the best people to teach us natural family planning, because it is nothing more than self-control out of love for each other." And what this poor person said is very true. These poor people maybe have nothing to eat, maybe they have no home to live in, but they can still be great people when they are spiritually rich. Those who are materially poor can be wonderful people. One evening we went out and we picked up four people from the street. And one of them was in a most terrible condition. I told the Sisters: "You take care of the other three; I will take care of the one who looks worse." So I did for her all that my love can do. I put her in bed, and there was a beautiful smile on her face. She took hold of my hand, and she said one thing only: "Thank you." Then she died.

I could not help but examine my conscience before her. I asked, "What would I say if I were in her place?" And my answer was very simple. I would have tried to draw a little attention to myself. I would have said, "I am hungry, I am dying, I am cold, I am in pain," or something like that. But she gave me much more—she gave me her grateful love. And she died with a smile on her face.

Then there was the man we picked up from the drain, half-eaten by worms. And after we had brought him to the home, he only said, "I have lived like an animal in the street, but am going to die as an angel, loved and cared for." Then, after we had removed all the worms from this body, all he said—with a big smile—was: "Sister, I am going home to God." And he died. It was so wonderful to see the greatness of that man, who could speak like that without blaming anybody, without comparing anything. Like an angel—this is the greatness of people who are spiritually rich, even when they are materially poor.

And so here I am talking with you. I want you to find the poor here, right in your own home first. And begin love there. Bear the good news to your own people first. And find out about your next-door neighbors. Do you know who they are?

I had the most extraordinary experience of love of a neighbor from a Hindu family. A gentleman came to our house and said, "Mother Teresa, there is a family who have not eaten for so long. Do something." So I took some rice and went there immediately. And I saw the children, their eyes shining with hunger. (I don't know if you have ever seen hunger, but I have seen it very often.) And the mother of the family took the rice I gave her, and went out. When she came back, I asked her, "Where did you go? What did you do?" And she gave me a very simple answer: "They are hungry also." What struck me was that she knew. And who were "they?" A Muslim family. And she knew. I didn't bring any more rice that evening, because I wanted them—Hindus and Muslims—to enjoy the joy of sharing.

Because I talk so much of giving with a smile, once a professor from the United States asked me, "Are you married?" And I said, "Yes, and I find it sometimes very difficult to smile at my spouse—Jesus—because he can be very demanding. Sometimes this is really something true. And there is where love comes in—when it is demanding, and yet we can give it with joy.

If we remember that God loves us, and that we can love others as he loves us, then America can become a sign of peace for the world. From here, a sign of care for the weakest of the weak—the unborn child—must go out to the world. If you become a burning light of justice and peace in the world, then really you will be true to what the founders of this country stood for. God bless you!

— Mother Teresa

A Mother's Tale:
A Story of Love, Forgiveness, and Life

In the early morning hours of May 31, 1999, the lives of two families and countless others were changed forever. Brian Muha, eighteen, and Aaron Land, twenty, both students of Franciscan University in Steubenville, Ohio, were kidnapped from their apartment, taken to a remote section of U.S. Route 22, brutally beaten, and each shot once in the head.

For the four days following their disappearance, family and friends waited in agony, holding on to hope as police searched for the boys. Within twenty-four hours following the kidnapping and murders, two suspects were arrested after being spotted driving Brian's missing Chevy Blazer, and a third turned himself in.

Later trials revealed that the motive for the murders was the Blazer. In the following three days, details began to come from the suspects, and on Friday, June 4, the bodies were found, confirming Rachel Muha's worst fear: her son Brian had been murdered.

But the story of the Muha family is not one of hatred, revenge, and death. It is one of love, forgiveness, and life. This faith response of Rachel and Chris Muha (Brian's older brother, then nineteen) began before they even knew he had been killed.

Following the disappearance of Brian and Aaron, the campus of Franciscan University was in shock. Students packed Christ the King Chapel on campus three times a day for prayer services. But on that Wednesday evening, those gathered heard two words from Rachel Muha that had the power to move mountains.

"I forgive," she said. "Whoever is responsible for what has happened to Brian and Aaron, and whatever you have done to them, I forgive you." When she learned of the brutality of her son's murder, she renewed her forgiveness. When the killers bragged in prison about what they had done, she renewed her forgiveness. And when they showed no remorse until the sentencing phase of their trials, she renewed her forgiveness. In fact, Rachel did more than just forgive the men who were bragging in prison about killing her son; she went to the district attorney and asked him not to seek the death penalty for the perpetrators, Terrell Yarbrough and Nathan Herring, both eighteen at the time.

Rachel Muha, in her victim's impact statement at the sentencing hearing, said that the death penalty in general should not be an option, though she acknowledged that some prisoners needed to be isolated for the safety of other prisoners.

The death penalty was not the only thing Rachel and Chris Muha spoke of in court. They also spoke directly to Herring and Yarbrough about salvation. "After this life, Nathan, each of us will go to heaven or hell," Rachel said. "As long as you are on this earth, you can choose. Choose heaven, Nathan. I'm praying for you. God bless you, Nathan."

She told Yarbrough, "Terrell, our lives are emptier, sadder, and lonelier. We can't have Brian and Aaron back, not the way we were used to. Your life can be emptier, sadder and lonelier than it has been, but it doesn't have to be. That's up to you. Turn to God, Terrell, and you can live a happy life, even in prison."

Chris also addressed Yarbrough, saying, "Terrell, I offer my forgiveness to you. I forgive you, not because you had a rough childhood, for that is not an excuse. I forgive you, not because you were depressed, because that is not an excuse. I forgive you because I have been forgiven. And I want so much to believe that you are truly sorry for what you have done."

Rachel explained that throughout the whole ordeal a multitude of graces were showered down on her from the Blessed Mother. She recalled the phone call from the Steubenville police that Monday afternoon.

"When I got the phone call and heard the voice say, 'Mrs. Muha, this is Detective Lelless from the Steubenville Police. Your son Brian is missing,' I had three great hopes: first, that we would find Brian alive; second, that I could see and hold my Brian again, alive or not; and third, that if I couldn't have Brian back alive, that I could see the place where he met Our Lord."

"Well," she continued, "Brian is not alive, not on earth—but he is in heaven and that gives me the greatest happiness. I did not get to see or hold my Brian one more time, and that gives me great sorrow and pain—my arms still ache. But I did get to go to the place where he died. I climbed the hill that Brian climbed and kissed the ground where Brian died, and there is a beautiful canopy of wild roses that are over the spot that I know were a gift from our Blessed Mother, and that is a great consolation."

Chris told of a second sign from Mary that brought his mother so much comfort. "Brian had returned to Steubenville from home in Columbus only the day before he was killed. Brian asked me if I could be home that Monday morning because he was going to have flowers sent for mom that morning and wanted to make sure I was there to get them in case she wasn't.

"When we got the flowers about 9:30 that morning, I read the note that said, 'Just wanted to say hi even though I'm away. Love, Brian.' When I read it, I had a strange feeling Brian was gone for a really long time. Detective Lelless called about five hours later telling us that Brian was missing and that there was blood in the house."

The third moment of grace came when the Muhas learned what Yarbrough was wearing around his neck when he was arrested: Brian's rosary. It is unknown how Yarbrough came into possession of the Rosary. But Rachel feels that whether he took it from Brian because he was praying or whether Brian gave it to him in his last minutes, Mary was there in his hour of death.

She told Yarbrough at the sentencing about the Rosary and how to pray it. "Brian and Aaron had weapons too. Powerful weapons. More powerful than your weapon. You didn't even know that what you had around your neck was more powerful than what you had in your hand. It's more powerful because it leads us to heaven where everything is beautiful. You can have this weapon in prison, if you like."

In his apostolic letter entitled *On the Christian Meaning of Human Suffering,* Pope John Paul II says that what makes human suffering specifically human is the question *why.* Since the funerals of Brian and Aaron and the trials of Herring and Yarbrough, Rachel Muha has begun a campaign to bring good out of the suffering of her son.

In the fall of 1999, she established the Brian Muha Memorial Foundation. "The whole reason to have the foundation and do this work is to help make the children of the area feel safe and free," Rachel says. "We know that to make a lasting change in a person's life he or she has to have love, discipline, a good moral education and a good academic education. We are committed, in Brian's and Aaron's names, to help ensure that."

According to Chris, the foundation raises money for the Brian Muha-Aaron Land Scholarship Fund at Franciscan University and for support of projects and programs in inner-city Steubenville, Columbus, and Pittsburgh.

"The scholarship is for students from inner-city Steubenville, Columbus, or Pittsburgh to go to Franciscan University who couldn't otherwise afford it," Chris said. "Brian was from Columbus, while Terrell and Nathan were from Pittsburgh and Steubenville." The major foundation fundraiser each summer is a golf outing. The first year, 142 golfers turned out and $37,000 was raised.

Rachel purchased the house the students were kidnapped from to use as a rent-free guest home for priests and others with religious vocations who are studying at the university. She said she bought the house, 150 miles from her suburban Columbus home, both to maintain its connection to her son and to defeat the evil that once raged there.

Rachel and Chris Muha hope their story of forgiveness will be a lesson to all. "You can't go through something like this and come out of it whole without God," says Rachel. "It's too traumatic and it's such a shock. Forgiveness is something God gives us for ourselves as well as for those we have to forgive. Forgiveness is a choice, and it's a choice I have to continue to make every day of my life."

— Nick Thomm

Nick Thomm is a journalist and executive producer of Kresta in the Afternoon, *a Catholic talk-radio program produced by Ave Maria Radio.*

A graduate of Franciscan University and classmate of Brian Muha, he also serves as a fill-in host for Ave Maria programs and has worked as a reporter for both Catholic and secular newspapers. He resides in Ann Arbor, Michigan with his wife, Jen.

Chapter 7

Expect the Unexpected

Andrew's Gift

Gathered around the dinner table one snug December evening, my husband, Bob, and I challenged our six children to think of ways to surprise people with random acts of kindness. Christmas was just around the corner, so our goal was to instill a true spirit of giving.

The kids thought a moment, then offered their ideas: "If there was someone new at school who didn't know anyone, I could make him feel welcome ... I could do someone's chore or make her bed ... How about shoveling a person's sidewalk and not telling him ... If I saw an old person leaving the grocery store with bags, I could offer to carry the bags to the car."

Everyone had contributed at least one idea for performing a random act of kindness. "I think they got it," I thought as I cleared the dishes.

A few days later when Luke, age nine, came home from his CCD class, a big grin announced that he had something special to tell me. "You know how we talked about random acts of kindness," Luke began. "I did one today!" He proceeded to tell me how his teacher, Mrs. Morrell, had given all her students a wrapped Christmas gift. As he held the little gift and recalled our conversation, I had an inspiration.

"I asked her if she had a son," Luke explained. "When she said, 'yes' I told her to give it to him."

My heart warmed with pleasure at my son's desire to show kindness to a boy he had never met. "Honey, that is so nice," I said hugging him.

That evening, the phone rang. "It's Mrs. Morrell and she wants to talk to you," one of the kids whispered. It crossed my mind that perhaps Luke's well-meaning gesture had been misunderstood. Was Mrs. Morrell hurt when Luke returned her gift?

"This is Mary Morrell, your son's CCD teacher," she began. To my relief, she expressed appreciation for Luke's generosity. "Luke asked me if I have a son and I told him, 'yes,'" Mrs. Morrell continued. "What I did not tell him was that our son, Andrew, died in a car accident several years ago when he was twenty-one."

My heart dropped and tears stung my eyes. I listened to the account of the loss of her dear Andrew (ironically the name of Luke's twin). I immediately felt a close bond with this woman whom I had never met. I felt like her son Andrew was someone our children could look up to. Carefully, I searched for the right words to express sympathy and my concern that Luke's action may have caused her pain.

"Oh, no," Mrs. Morrell reassured me. "As a matter of fact, every year I put a Christmas ornament on Andrew's grave. The gift I gave to Luke was an ornament. I would like that to be the one I put on Andrew's grave this year." She paused for a moment and then asked, "Do you think he would like to come with you and your family and be the one to give it to Andrew?"

Delighted to be included at such a special moment, I accepted the invitation. The next week, Luke, three of the other children, and I gathered at St. Agnes' Cemetery. Despite the cold afternoon air, I think we all felt a warm glow when greeted by Mrs. Morrell's peaceful smile and sincere embrace.

We walked a short distance to Andrew's grave site. Mrs. Morrell passed out candy canes and Christmas treats to the kids. Then, holding up a snapshot of a young man, she introduced us all to her beloved Andy with stories of his kindness to others.

"Would you like to be the one to put this year's ornament on his grave?" Mrs. Morrell asked Luke. He carefully took the stained glass ornament and placed it alongside the others. Then we all held hands and prayed before walking back to our cars.

I think my children shared in the good feeling I had as we drove home. Not only had Luke's random act of kindness reached out in Christian love to someone here on earth, but now we felt connected with someone who had gone before us.

After the holidays, I was waiting at our church, St. Maximilian Kolbe, for one of my little athletes to finish up with basketball practice. To pass the time, I glanced through the Catholic Youth Organization trophy case outside the gym. A plaque for outstanding achievement and good sportsmanship for parish teens caught my eye. Scanning the brass plated names, I thought to myself, "How nice to recognize young people for being good to others."

This plaque had obviously been in the trophy case for several years, but I was reading it for the first time. I looked to the top of the plaque and caught my breath as I read the heading: "Andrew Morrell Award."

"Thank you Andy," I thought, "You have given us much."

— Pinky McGreevy

Pinky McGreevy, homemaker and mom of six children (ages 10 to 17), resides in West Chester, Pennsylvania. She has served as a volunteer for numerous school and church positions, including PTO president of the local elementary school. With five football players on five different teams, as well as one cheerleader, this busy mom can be seen daily doing one of her favorite things—driving the family's conversion van around town as a "taxi" for many sporting and social events.

The Man Who Gave All

Abe Joseph, a stocky young man with a trimmed short beard on a warm, smiling face, strolled through the juvenile center scrutinizing the extensive remodeling. He carried numerous papers containing architectural plans, along with his own drawings and designs.

Abe was the executive director of the center, determined to make the building comfortable and attractive to the community's youngsters. He sat in his office working on the figures of the costs involved, trying somehow to keep within the budget. The sum they had was the best they could raise so far in the community, but he worried if they had undertaken too large a project. A tap on the locked door interrupted his concentration. An elderly man stood behind the glass-topped door.

"Hello, may I help you?" Abe asked.

"What is the building for?" the gentleman asked. "I see construction going on."

"If we ever get it completed, it will be a community center for youngsters to get together and stay away from all the bad influences out there today."

The old gent nodded. "Ah, good." He leaned toward Abe and continued. "May I go through it, please?"

Surprised by the request, Abe hesitated, knowing how much work he still had to do before leaving for the day. However, the man appeared lonely and Abe's compassion took over.

"Well, yes, I'll give you a tour of our facility," he said as he rose and led the elderly man out of the office. It proved to be a slow process: The man walked with a cane and did not seem well. Abe gave him a complete tour. He was amazed that the man, in an obviously weakened condition, wanted to walk through the entire building.

"We're not certain that we can include all we need here," Abe explained, "as we're in a money bind. It's a poor neighborhood, and the people have donated whatever they could. If I had a little extra, I'd run a fund-raising affair—you know, dinner and entertainment. Perhaps that would do it. Anyway, we'll do the best that we can."

"Thank you, young man, you're very kind," the elderly gentlemen said. "Not many people take time out for us old folks. Bless you."

A week later a letter addressed to "The kind young man in the office" arrived at the center. Abe opened the envelope.

"For your kindness in taking time from your work to indulge an old man's curiosity, please accept the enclosed donation to help with the work, or to run your fund-raising party." At the bottom was an additional note:

This note was written by Jane Smith for Mr. Michael Berley, who had a critical stroke. Prior to his death, Mr. Berley requested this be taken care of. It is all the money he had in the world, and although it is a small amount, he hoped it would bring good luck.

Deeply touched, Abe felt a tightness in his throat as he unfolded the check. He gasped—$2,500. The dinner party would surely carry them over the top.

The party flyers read: *In Memory of Michael Berley.*

— Florence J. Paul

Florence Paul, from Santa Ana, California, is an award-winning author of five books and many articles. She has two children, three grandchildren, and one great-grandchild.

One Last Mass

On my journey back to God and religion, I attended a candle lighting service with my husband, Gene, at his Baptist church a few days before Christmas. It seemed right to stick together in this journey, to find a common ground in one denomination. And I knew, with his strong Baptist upbringing, that Gene was not about to become Catholic.

That night in the Baptist church just happened to be one of the rare occasions where they celebrated what they term "The Lord's Supper." My husband reminded me that the Eucharist was just a symbol and that I could not partake until I became Baptist. That was fine with me, of course, because I had long ago forgotten anyone mentioning the Church's belief in Christ's real presence in the Eucharist. An usher began passing the plate of little symbolic bread across from the left ... the side I was on. As the man at my side prepared to hand it off to me, the plate literally flew out of my hands, into the air. Gene scrambled to catch it. Just as he caught the plate, the little cubes of bread fell back onto it. Needless to say, I was so embarrassed I wanted to crawl under the pew. It disquieted me so much that I could not shake the feeling that just maybe I should attend one last nostalgic midnight Mass just to be certain I should become a Baptist.

The following Saturday was Christmas Eve. From childhood memories I knew there was always confession on Saturday afternoon. I decided I should go to confession as I had been taught to do growing up. I wanted to properly prepare for this "last Mass." As I entered the church, there was no one around but a workman putting up decorations. I could not figure out where the confessional was and he evidently saw my confusion. When he asked if I needed help, I explained I was there for confession. Giving me a strange look he replied: "Confessions have already finished for today. We are getting ready for midnight Mass."

My face flushed with embarrassment. "Sorry," I said. "I'll just be going. Thanks so much for your help!" I was pretty sure the man must have pegged me correctly as what my father called "A Christmas Cactus and an Easter Lily." I turned to leave as fast as I could, deciding to forget the whole thing and just get on with becoming a Baptist.

As I rushed toward the side door, I ran smack into what I assumed was another workman. He grabbed my arm to keep me from falling and asked, "Can I help you?"

"Oh! No, I was leaving," I stammered. "I thought there were confessions at 4 p.m. I'll just be on my way."

Then, out of his back pocket came a Roman collar. "Come on," he said directing me to the confessional. "I'm Father Mike." I was too dumbfounded to do anything other than follow through with my original plan.

That night at the Mass, I was filled with such peace. As I joined the communion line, I truly felt God was blessing my sincere seeking of His will. All the way toward the front of the church, I concentrated on how to receive the Eucharist. Things had changed a lot over the past twenty years. I was a bit nervous about the fact there was no longer an altar rail. I was very busy trying to listen and learn the seemingly new rubrics from those ahead of me in line. I did not want to be embarrassed again. I thought: "That looks easy ... place one hand on the other ... say 'Amen!' to whatever the priest is saying to you ... take the host, eat and off I go ... No problem!"

As I placed my cupped hands to receive the host, I had the overwhelming feeling that this little host was not just a bread cube. It felt extremely heavy in my hand. I stumbled and hit the floor on my knees. I was once again so embarrassed and confused I wanted to disappear. Until, that is, I heard a still, small Voice say to me, "It is I, your Jesus. I was not in the Lord's Supper. I am here. Welcome home!"

I returned to my seat very spiritually shaken. The rest of Mass was a blur to say the least! I felt very confused, blessed and very unworthy. And so my journey home began.

God writes straight with crooked lines and in the following days, weeks and years I would learn just how faithful and loving He is. I now knew without any doubt, that as unworthy as I might be, I was called home to my Catholic roots.

— Christine Trollinger

Christine Trollinger is the author of several of the stories in this book. Her biographical information appears after The Badge of Grace *in Chapter One.*

Refueling with God

My heart leaped with joy upon learning I had just landed a job as manager at a gas station in Pella, Iowa. To some, it might seem like an odd vocation for a college graduate, but for one seeking to evangelize, a gas station was fertile ground. People from all walks of life—Christian and non-Christian—would be walking through the door of the station. I would be there to meet them, get to know them, and look for opportunities to lead them to Christ.

I had just recently quit my job as an announcer at a Christian radio station. Instead of preaching to the choir, I yearned to get out into the world and evangelize among people who did not know Christ.

The job turned out to be everything I had hoped it would be. By being friendly and interested in people, I got to know many of the regular customers. There had been many opportunities to befriend people, listen to their problems, and often lead them closer to Christ.

I came to enjoy my early morning routine at the station. Arriving at 5 a.m. to do inventory each morning provided me with quiet time to pray and reflect before opening at 6 a.m. On one such morning, I was surprised to see a customer at the pump just after I opened.

As I watched the young man pump gas into his car, I suddenly had the strong impression that I should say something to him about Jesus when he walked in to pay. Now, even though this was the reason I was working at the gas station, it was not my style to hit people with Christianity in such a direct manner. I had worked there three months and had never done anything like that. I usually befriended people over time and got to know them before sharing my faith with them.

When the thought first came to me, I said to the Lord: "I don't want to do this. It's not the normal way to greet people. I don't want to seem weird." Yet, as I watched this professional looking man in a business suit, the feeling grew stronger that God wanted me to say something to him such as, "Sir, Jesus loves you."

I argued with God: "Lord, let me get to know him first, then I'll say something." But the feeling only grew stronger. I had the impression that if I did not do this, I would be disobedient to what the Lord was asking of me.

Although I am not the nervous type, I started getting nervous. The man looked "no-nonsense" and appeared to be in a hurry. He paced about while he waited for his tank to fill.

I thought, "If this feeling is from the Lord, there is only one way I'm going to know and that is to go ahead and say something." I was reminded of the apostles in the boat when they saw Jesus walking across the water to them. They were afraid and thought he was a ghost. Jesus comforted them and assured them it was him. Peter said, "Lord if it is you, ask me to walk on the water." Peter then proceeded to get out of the boat, probably much to the surprise of the other apostles. As Peter put one leg out of the boat, he must have been wondering the same thing I was wondering that morning: "Is that really God?" Like Peter, the only way I was going to know if this feeling was coming from God was to get out of the boat.

The guy finished filling his car and made his way to the station. I swallowed hard as he opened the door.

Forcing myself to look him in the eyes, I took a deep breath and said, "Sir, Jesus loves you."

There was a silent pause that seemed to last an eternity. The man looked puzzled but then anger clouded his face. I became even more nervous imagining that he might come across the counter and knock me out. But then, he stopped and shook his head back and forth as if to say, "What is going on here?"

The man then proceeded to tell me that even though it was only six in the morning, already four people had told him that day that Jesus loved him. "What is going on?" he asked.

"Well", I answered, "maybe God is speaking to you." He then softened and explained that he had stopped walking with the Lord some time ago and perhaps God was calling him back home. We stood there in silence for a moment before he thanked me and said, "This has given me something to think about." He then turned and left.

I never saw him again but I prayed that the hound of heaven would continue to chase him until he gave his life to Christ. I may never know what happened in the end but I do know that he encountered the love of God that day. I pray that I will meet him one day in heaven.

God gives us all opportunities to preach the gospel and share His love, but with that opportunity there comes risk. If we will respond to that risk in faith and love, we will be surprised what God can do through us.

— Jeff Cavins

Providential Preservatives

The Little Things

Scanning the shelves at a used bookstore, my eyes came to rest on a book entitled *The Dreyfuss Affair*. I pulled it out and scanned the back-cover synopsis. I had run across references to Dreyfuss many times in my readings, a French soldier who had been accused of spying in the late 1800s. His trial had been a controversial one and I was intrigued by the story.

I purchased the book thinking it would give me something to read that night. I was driving home from a business trip in Washington, DC to Steubenville, Ohio, and needed to spend the night at a hotel.

The book turned out to be a page turner. It was on my mind as I got ready early the next morning. "Now this is a story that would make a great movie," I thought while showering. "And that actor with the same name ... what's his first name? Richard? Richard Dreyfuss? Yeah, that's it. He'd be perfect for the part," I determined.

Getting dressed, I clicked on the TV and switched to a random movie. The actors were dressed as French soldiers. Richard Dreyfuss suddenly appeared. He was being accused of spying. Goosebumps covered me—it was a movie about the Dreyfuss affair, starring Richard Dreyfuss!

Everyone has these instances in life, coincidences which defy any explanation. We are often tempted to try to make sense out of them. Instead, I have come to believe that when the seemingly impossible occurs in minor or insignificant instances, it is just God smiling, saying: "Hey, I'm here with you."

During this time, there were a number of areas in my life I was trying to sort out. It seemed my prayers were not being answered. The seemingly insignificant yet incredible coincidence in the hotel room gave me reassurance—God was with me. He was smiling.

In my life, most of the moments of grace that have impacted me completely lose their power in the telling. Most people write them off as coincidences. Yet I have found that it is through the little things that God communicates that He is very near.

There was the time when I went skiing and lost a contact lens at the very top of a steep, snowy slope. Without my contacts, I am nearly blind—I could not safely ski without my lens. I prayed for God to help me, knelt in the snow, and found it. If I had jumped up announcing to everyone that God had just found my contact for me, the ski patrol would have carted me down the slope in a straight jacket. But the odds of finding a tiny, clear contact in the snow assured me that God had heard my prayer.

On another occasion, I had the feeling I needed to return to the parking to get a book I had left in my car. It was raining and it was not essential that I have the book right then, but still, the feeling that I should get the book nagged at me. I gave in to the feeling and returned to my car. When I inserted the key, I stepped on something. It was my wallet. I must have dropped on the ground earlier.

Too often people say, "Wasn't I lucky?" or "What a coincidence!" or even "Ain't I clever!" But when we have come to the place in our spiritual journey when our first instinct is to respond "That was Jesus!" and "Thank you, Lord," then we can be reassured that our hardened hearts have been converted by the grace of our loving God.

In his classic work, *Introduction to the Devout Life*, St. Frances de Sales speaks about the importance of recognizing God's inspirations in our everyday lives. We tend to be more aware of *temptations* and often miss out on the *inspirations*. We miss them because they are so ordinary— yet they are not.

It reminds me of my favorite Bible passage: "Trust in the Lord with all your heart, and lean not onto your own understanding. In all your ways acknowledge him, and he will make straight your paths" (Proverbs 3:5-6).

God is always with us. If our hearts are open to Him and to hearing His sometimes still small voice, we will see that He reveals Himself to us everyday of our lives.

— Marcus Grodi

Marcus Grodi is the host of the television program, The Journey Home, *and the founder and president of the Coming Home Network, a non-profit apostolate that assists non-Catholics, both clergy and laity, on their journeys into the Catholic faith. A convert himself, Marcus speaks regularly at parishes and conferences on a variety of Catholic issues.*

Treated to a Blessing

Walking out into a crisp September afternoon, my mood soared. My co-workers and I had just completed the first milestone of a very important and complicated project. As an energy and environmental comfort specialist, I had sold a product for renovating the heating, cooling, lighting, and indoor air quality for a 220,000 square-foot, ten-story office building in Norristown, Pennsylvania.

"This deserves a celebration," I thought to myself as I walked into the convenience store next-door. As I looked at the shelves for something to treat myself to, a thought came to me: "Someone needs this more than I do"

It was not as if I was down to my last dollar and had to choose between buying myself something or giving to charity, but the thought seemed to be a direction—a prompting. Recently, I seem to be getting more direction from God in my life since I changed my morning prayer routine. My new routine involves sitting quietly and trying to be fully present to the Lord, to be open to what He wants me to do. I am no mystic. I do not hear audible voices, but I sense that this morning spiritual exercise has helped me to be more in tune with God's plan for me each day.

On this particular day, it would have been easy for me to brush the thought away and go ahead and buy myself a candy bar or cupcake. After all, the idea that interrupted my confectionary plans seemed totally subjective. I could choose to listen to this soft prodding or brush it aside. I turned on my heels and left the store.

Back outside, there were street maintenance vehicles and personnel working nearby. I watched what they were doing for a few minutes. A man alongside me explained that a transformer had blown up the day before. The crew was working on the repair.

As we were watching the scene, another man walked up to me and asked, "Can you spare fifty cents?" The middle-aged man looked homeless. He carried his belongings in a bag. He had probably slept outside on some park bench or in some doorway entrance. Despite his appearance, you could see that he was probably new to living on the streets. He was certainly down on his luck, but perhaps it was only a temporary situation. He had a pleading look in his eyes as he quietly said, "Even a dime would help."

I reached into my pocket, and pulled out a twenty-dollar bill and gave it to him. The man looked at the bill and then back up at me, obviously surprised. Looking me square in the eyes, he said, "Thank you! You do not know how important this is to me." He then turned and walked away with a livelier step than he had approached. I watched him pump his fist and mouth, "Yes!" That look in his eyes and that gesture of excitement gave me much more satisfaction than any treat could ever have offered.

The man standing next to me watched a moment, then commented dryly: "You could stand here all day and do that."

"Yes, I think I could" I agreed. "And maybe that is what the Lord wants me to do."

— Bob McGreevy

Bob McGreevy is the husband of Pinky McGreevy, whose story Andrew's Gift *appears at the beginning of this chapter. He is a '75 Notre Dame graduate (and fullback) and a mechanical engineer. Bob, father of six, has been a youth football coach for twenty-five years, and served as co-chairman of the building committee of St. Maximilian Kolbe parish in West Chester, Pennsylvania.*

Will the Real Progressive Please Stand Up?

More than a century ago, a proud university student boarded a train in France and sat next to an older man who seemed to be a peasant of comfortable means. The brash student noticed that the older gentleman was slipping beads through his fingers. He was praying the Rosary.

"Sir, do you still believe in such outdated things?" the student inquired. "Yes, I do. Don't you?" the man responded. The student laughed and admitted, "I do not believe in such silly things. Take my advice. Throw that rosary out the window and learn what science has to say about it."

"Science? I do not understand this science. Perhaps you can explain it to me," the man said humbly, tears welling in his eyes.

The university student noticed that the man was deeply moved. To avoid hurting the older person's feelings, he said, "Please give me your address and I will send you some literature to explain the matter to you."

The man fumbled in the inside pocket of his coat and pulled out his business card. On reading the card, the student lowered his head in shame and was speechless. The card read: "Louis Pasteur, Director of the Institute of Scientific Research, Paris." The deluded student had encountered his country's leading chemist; indeed, one of the greatest scientists the world has ever known.

— Br. John Samaha, S.M.

Brother John Samaha is a retired brother of the Society of Mary congregation. He writes articles and lives in Cupertino, California.

Vehicle to Priesthood

My first memory is of the crucifix in my boyhood parish, Holy Name in Birmingham, Michigan. I do not know how old I was, but I knew Jesus had died for me and my whole life was supposed to be a response to this.

This is certainly not a typical first memory but my family was anything but typical. My father, John, was the chief executive officer and chairman of the board of Chrysler Corporation, and also a devout Catholic. He proved that religion was not just a crutch for the weak. Every night he was on his knees before he went to bed, and even during his frequent travels he went to daily Mass. My mother, Thelma, was born a Methodist, but she accompanied us to Mass long before her eventual conversion to the Catholic faith. God was ever present in our family.

I was the youngest of five children and my very existence occurred against the advice of my mother's doctor, because of her painful and crippling back condition. My mom later told me that I was a gift to her and my father, and in turn, they gave me back to God.

During my childhood, my prayers centered around my mother's bad back. Endless treatments failed to alleviate her constant pain. When I was thirteen, one of my sisters called our mother to tell her she had just come from a charismatic prayer meeting and someone had sensed that God wanted to cure someone with a bad back. My sister was convinced it would be our mother. Within a month, mom was playing tennis—completely healed—although there was no medical reason for the pain to be gone. Two years later, she formally converted to the Catholic faith.

Growing up in this home of prayer and miracles gave me a strong anchor. Yet, ironically, as a teenager, I began to hide my faith. I never stopped praying, but I no longer went to confession. By the time I attended the University of Michigan in Ann Arbor, my attendance at Mass was sporadic. It wasn't enjoyable to hear the Gospel when I was not living a holy life.

Not until my junior year in college, in 1986, did my life change. I began connecting with a group of young men for basketball games who were part of an ecumenical Christian brotherhood outreach group. I saw men my own age who were normal guys but really knew God and were not afraid to talk about it. I began to examine my life and went through a conversion. At this time, I broke off a serious romance, leaving me free to concentrate on Christian outreach to university students.

Upon graduation, armed with a degree in English and communications, I interviewed for jobs in the automotive industry. It soon became clear to me that this was not the life God intended for me. So while trying to find my niche in the world, I accepted a job baking bread. With great trepidation, I drove home to tell my father of my plans to bake bread. I thought my dad would be disappointed. Instead, he told me he would be thrilled with whatever I chose to do in life, even if I wanted to be a priest. I assured him that would never happen.

Driving back to Ann Arbor that day, tears streamed down my face as I felt my life was moving beyond my own control. I wanted to follow Jesus, but as yet I was unclear where that led. What I was suddenly clear on, however, was that following Jesus was not going to be easy; the Cross is heavy. I realized I was not the one in control.

As I cried, the words to a Christian song, "God's Own Fool" played on my car stereo. " ... So come lose your life for a carpenter's son, for a madman who died for a dream. And you'll have the faith His first followers had and you'll feel the weight of the beam."

At that very moment, I had an actual vision of our Lord in my car. He sat next to me. It was clear that it was Him. He reached across the seat and dug his right hand into my chest and said, 'John, these are all your dreams, goals, desires, and everything you want to do with your life.' He withdrew His hand and pulled everything out and motioned throwing it all out the window. I said, 'Lord, that's my life you just threw out the window.' Jesus then said, 'John, I'm going to give you my dream, my goal, my desire and what I want you to do with your life.' And then He was gone."

Suddenly I felt panicked. This was so personal. Still, I did not know what God had planned for me. For the next three years, I did Christian outreach with university students. For a time I seriously considered joining a Christian non-denominational brotherhood, but ultimately decided it was not for me.

By the time I was twenty-five, I took a job in Ohio working for Ford Motor in an account management training program. I was dating again and had decided to apply to graduate school. During this time, while reading my Bible one day, I came across this passage in Matthew: "Some are incapable of marriage because they were born so; some, because they were made so by others; some, because they have renounced marriage for the sake of the kingdom of heaven. Whoever can accept this ought to accept it."

Something stirred within me. I thought, "Oh nuts! I think I'm supposed to do this.'" I almost threw my Bible on the ground. In frustration, I cried out to God, "Lord, I don't get it. I thought of marriage once, that didn't fit; the brotherhood didn't fit, I started dating again, that didn't fit ... "

Suddenly, I heard a clear voice speaking to me: "John, I'm inviting you to live single and to do it as a priest." Although the voice would not have been audible to another, it was certainly not my own voice—I had never even considered the priesthood.

I responded, "Lord, if that's what You want me to do, then You better give me a desire for it, because I don't have it." Five days went by, and I longed to know more about the priesthood.

It was late December in 1990 when I contacted the vocation director of Sacred Heart Seminary in Detroit. I had to wait until the next school year to be admitted, but in the meantime I could take a few classes. As I walked into the building for the first time, a wave of peace washed over me. I thought, "I'm finally home." I knew with full clarity that this was what God was calling me to. I realized that this was why I was made—an amazing thing to grasp.

After a year-and-a-half at Sacred Heart, I was asked to finish my theological studies in Rome. Before final admission to the North American College, I needed a physical. Although in excellent physical condition and only twenty-six, tests indicated possible heart irregularities. A stress test was scheduled. After studying the results, the cardiologist questioned me about any severe childhood illnesses I may have had. There had been high fevers and seizures but nothing more.

"No, that couldn't have done it," the doctor determined and told me that I had unexplainable scar tissue on my heart. The prognosis was that it was nothing to be concerned about but it could occasionally cause shortness of breath.

I had been in Rome for a month when I was in chapel one day meditating on the three pivotal moments in my life: my first memory of the crucifix, the vision in the car, and the invitation to be a priest. It was at that moment when it became clear to me, where the scar tissue on my heart had come from. I felt like God told me, 'The scar tissue is from my hand.'"

I have been a priest now for eight great, though challenging, years. Often, during the Mass, at the moment of consecration, when I lift the bread and wine and it becomes the Body and Blood of Our Lord Jesus Christ, I often lose my breath and feel as if my heart is being squeezed. It is a reminder to me of the day God "barged" into my life and brought me to the joy of the priesthood.

— Fr. John Ricardo

Fr. John Ricardo works at St. John's Center for Youth and Family in Plymouth, Michigan. He is the director of the Cardinal Maida Institute.

Tonsure in the Tulips

An Undivided Heart

I'm sure the day will dawn bright and early...perhaps a little too early, as my flight departs at sunrise. A mixture of emotions floods through me as I contemplate the new chapter of life that is opening before me. As I write this, I am preparing to leave my hometown of Hebron, in the beautiful state of North Dakota, to set out on a journey that will change my life forever.

I leave behind many precious memories and wonderful people. Yet I look to the future with hope and joy—I am answering the Lord's call. The Lord has blessed me with the grace of a religious vocation as a Dominican sister of St. Cecilia in Nashville, Tennessee.

I am sometimes asked how I knew that I was called to be a sister. Growing up, I had no exposure to nuns or monks. The thought of a religious vocation had never entered my mind until my junior year of college. Looking back, however, I can see the Lord had been preparing me. I never quite fit in with my classmates, preferring quiet time alone with a good book. I naturally excelled in everything I did, yet I knew there had to be something more to life than academics, music, and sports. Although I knew little about my faith, it has always been important to me.

Upon entering college, I was given the grace of a Protestant boyfriend who questioned everything I believed. This forced me to really learn my faith. One summer, I worked at a children's camp in New York where I was told that if I talked about being Catholic, I would be fired. I was not able to attend Sunday Mass for nine weeks. It was through this time of being separated from the sacraments and other Catholics that I really learned to appreciate them.

I also began to see more clearly that the things of this world could never fulfill the longing in my heart for something more. Even when everything seemed so perfect, a little voice would speak to me in the silence of my heart asking, "Is this all there is to life?" I longed for something more, but I didn't know what that "more" could be.

I clearly remember the first time the thought of a religious vocation entered my mind. I was a junior in college and had just begun attending daily Mass. Since I was young, I had always planned on getting married, having many children, and seeing the world. But alone in my room one evening, I suddenly got the feeling that I was not supposed to get married. Well then, I thought, what am I doing to do with my life?

The answer that came to mind was, maybe I'm supposed to be a nun. I got a sinking feeling in my stomach similar to when you visit the dentist for a cavity and hear the drill start up. I pleaded, "Lord, I want to follow You, and I want to do your will for my life, but please don't make me be a nun." Then I simply prayed for the courage to follow His will and if He really did want me to be a nun to please give me the desire.

As time passed, I found that every once in a while, I thought about how wonderful it would be to have a religious vocation. Increasingly, there became more times that I liked the idea rather than fought it. One day, while praying, I realized that more than anything else in life, I wanted to completely dedicate myself to the Lord through religious life. The Lord had conformed my will to His.

Besides thinking that it's what God wants of me, why would I ever *want* to become a nun? Most people don't understand the religious vocation—why someone would choose to leave family, friends, and career—and even more than that, give up the freedom to make one's own choices. This lack of comprehension is understandable, as a religious vocation deals with something hard for us to grasp; it deals with pure joy—a joy so lofty and so deep that most simply have no concept of it. To be consecrated is to have an undivided heart—to have no desire except to love, praise, and glorify God and to follow His holy will. It's all about being in love.

Religious life is very similar to marriage, only Christ Himself is the divine Spouse. The call to religious life is a beautiful gift; as one sister I know says: "When the God of the universe asked me to become His spouse, how could I ever say no?"

So, must all people striving for holiness become priests or nuns? No. We must focus not on ourselves, but always on the Lord. Where is He calling you? The decision you must make is not the decision of what you think you want to do with your life, but rather whether you will follow the Lord's will.

To paraphrase the words of Pope John Paul II: "To everyone reading this, especially the young people—if you hear the Lord calling you, do not reject it! Dare to follow in the footsteps of the saints! Dare to become part of the great movements of holiness! Dare to follow Christ without reservations! Every day, every moment of every day, ask the Lord to give you the strength and courage to follow His most holy will. And if you hear the Lord inviting you to seek holiness in religious life, readily follow Mary's example by replying, 'Yes, Lord! Be it done unto me according to Thy word.'"

May the Lord give you the wisdom to discern His will for you, and the strength and courage to follow His plan for your life, wherever it may lead you. Praised be Jesus Christ, now and forever!

— Sr. Cecelia Anne Wanner, OP

Sr. Cecelia Anne Wanner took her first vows as a Nashville Dominican Sister in August, 2003.

Hailing Mary

My wife, Pat, and I made our first extended visit to Ireland in 1998. Early in April we took a side trip from Dublin to the small village of Knock. It is here that on August 21, 1879, fifteen people ranging in age from six to seventy-five, watched an apparition of the Blessed Mother with St. Joseph, St. John the Apostle, and the Lamb of God.

During our pilgrimage, Pat and I stayed at an old convent run as a bed-and-breakfast by the Sisters of Mercy. On this day, the sky was overcast but the weather was unusually dry. I had just purchased a container for holy water at one of the small shops lining the tiny main road in Knock. While Pat stayed back at our room, I went to collect the holy water from one of the wells set in a row framed by fieldstones and small water taps. As I passed the old church where the apparition of 1879 had taken place, I paused, reflecting on my rich spiritual life that had begun when I converted to Catholicism while attending a Jesuit prep school in California.

I had been through life's proverbial highs and lows for seventy years—hospitalized several times with life-threatening childhood asthma, severely wounded in combat during the Korean Conflict, survived heart attacks and many surgeries. I had a solid, enriching marriage which produced sons and many grandchildren. Although I was a devout Catholic, confident in our Lord, I suddenly pondered the fact that all my life, I had never had a distinct sign from heaven. My wife, also a convert, had three times received heavenly signs, including a loving, gentle voice that encouraged her to persevere through an especially arduous illness. "Why," I asked part thinking and part praying, "have I never been privileged to experience such divine confirmation?"

When I reached the well for holy water to bring back to share with family and friends, I bent to push the small buttoned tap releasing the blessed water. As I touched the button, I felt a "raining" on my head so I instinctively pulled up my jacket hood. Raising my eyes, my breath caught in my throat. There was no rain—only perfect little white hailstones the size of marbles. I watched them bounce off the well stones in front of me and felt them falling on my head. When I looked on either side of me and across the road I was amazed to realize the hailstones were falling only on me. There were none falling anywhere else in the area. The shower lasted perhaps twenty seconds and then stopped.

My thoughts did not crystallize at first other than feeling awe that I was the only one being touched by the unusual hail shower. I hurriedly finished filling the container, crossed the road and walked back to the convent room where my wife was meditating. As I entered the door, she looked up and saw something unusual in my expression.

"What is it?" she asked. "Are you okay?" After relating my story, Pat smiled knowingly and said, "*Hail*, Mary!"

It was at that moment that it hit me; I had received my sign.

— Richard Armstrong

Richard Armstrong, the father of three grown children, now lives in Eugene, Oregon. See the history and prayer of Our Lady of Knock on the next page.

History of Knock Shrine

In poverty-stricken Knock, Ireland, on August 21, 1879, fifteen people, ranging in age from six to seventy-five, watched an apparition of the Blessed Mother with St. Joseph, St. John the Apostle, and the Lamb of God. The vision lasted for two hours in the pouring rain. While all fifteen of the visionaries were soaked, no rain fell in the direction of the gable of St. John the Baptist Church, where the ground remained dry. All the witnesses testified to seeing the Blessed Virgin Mary clothed in white robes with a beautiful golden rose on her forehead and a brilliant crown upon her head. On her right stood St. Joseph and St. John was on her left. Behind them, on a plain altar, there appeared a cross with the Lamb, surrounded by angels. To this poverty-stricken area, this vision was a symbol of hope and consolation.

From the time the vision was first reported, pilgrims have been coming to the shrine, and hundreds of miraculous cures have been reported. In 1979, Pope John Paul II was among the pilgrims to Knock, confirming the status of the Knock shrine as one of the major Marian shrines in the world.

Prayer of Our Lady of Knock

Our Lady of Knock, Queen of Ireland, you gave hope to your people in a time of distress and comforted them in sorrow. You have inspired countless pilgrims to pray with confidence to your divine Son, remembering His promise: "Ask and you shall receive, seek and you shall find."

Help me to remember that we are all pilgrims on the road to heaven. Fill me with love and concern for my brothers and sisters in Christ, especially those who live with me. Comfort me when I am sick, lonely, or depressed. Teach me how to take part ever more reverently in the holy Mass. Pray for me now, and at the hour of my death. Amen.

Our Lady of Knock, pray for us.

Ernie the Adorer

I'll never forget my boyhood pet Ernie. Perhaps I did not mean as much to him as he did to me, but Ernie provided me with companionship. Also, I cannot say there never was another Ernie. There were actually several Ernies, each surviving about a year. That was about the maximum lifespan for the pet turtles I delighted in owning—each one named Ernie.

It was not unusual for Ernie to get lost in the house. I often freed him from his bowl to crawl around and see the world. Occasionally I lost track of him. At such times, even my sister helped with my frantic search for Ernie. But one day, despite looking under every piece of furniture and in every corner, Ernie remained missing.

When days passed and Ernie was still not found I thought: "Ernie must be dead wherever he is." I was sad, but preparations for the coming of Christmas distracted me from Ernie's absence.

One day, I noticed many of the Nativity figures under our Christmas tree were knocked over. I bent to straighten them. Much to my joyful surprise, there was Ernie sleeping next to Baby Jesus' manager. Good old Ernie! He knew where to go for comfort and safety.

— Br. John Raymond

Brother John Raymond's biography appears after Spot the Monk *in Chapter One.*

Intercessors in Iraq

Looking at the February 21 date on the calendar, my thoughts turned to my nephew, Andrew Anastasia. It was his birthday. I still remembered him as a cute little boy, getting into mischief. But he was now a twenty-one-year-old man. Andrew would probably not receive presents or celebrate in any big way because he was an Army reservist on active duty in the war with Iraq. I am sure his only birthday wish was to make it home alive.

Initially, our family was left in the dark as to where Andrew might be located in Iraq. There was an information blackout, for obvious reasons. Then we learned that his unit, the 459th, was attached to the First Marine Expeditionary Force, and we were able to figure out where he was located due to news stories about the Marine Force. Watching a report on television one night, my heart sank when I learned the ground war had become ugly where Andrew's unit was located.

"Dear Lord," I prayed, "please take care of Andrew. Send my own guardian angel to protect him and to comfort him."

My sister Terri, Andrew's mom, later informed me she too had asked God to send an army of angels to keep him and his unit safe. Talking with my other sisters and cousins, we realized we had all done the same thing—sent angels over to Andrew. There was nothing more we could do but pray and wait.

In late March, we discovered a website that contained news about Andrew's unit. I read intently that his unit was in the thick of combat, with a lot of rifle and missle fire between Iraq and the Allied Coalition. There were suicide bombers, and a heavy loss of Allied equipment. I was shocked as I read of the hundreds of dead bodies that members of Andrew's unit had counted on the sides of roads. Even though Andrew was a new reservist, he had seen more of the realities of war than most men had seen in other wars.

The commanding officer of Andrew's unit expressed the same thoughts—the surreal scene of so many dead bodies. It was more than he expected to face. Then, as I got to the bottom of one of the articles, I was filled with awe. The sergeants of the battalion agreed that something quasi-miraculous must have happened to protect the Allied Coalition's forces. They thought that God must have sent a battalion of angels to protect the 459th. Despite the heavy artillery fire they were under, there had not been a single injury. Tears filled my eyes. God had answered our pleas. Our angels had been on duty to protect our forces, and my nephew.

— Kathleen Tomasetti

Kathleen Tomasetti has spent the last sixteen years raising her three children. This never-before-published mom got her inspiration to write from the battalion of angels God sent to protect her nephew and his unit serving in Iraq. She and her family live in New Castle, Pennsylvania. Andrew, however, is still in Iraq and is not expected to return before January or February 2004. Notes of encouragement and support, as well as prayers for Andrew, can be sent to him at: Spc. Andrew Anastasia, Operation Enduring Freedom, First Bridge, 459th Eng. Co., Los Dogwood, Apo-AE-09302.

See pictures related to this story at www.AmazingGraceOnLine.net/Heart

My "Meating" with God

Driving home from my in-laws one Sunday evening in June, I could not shake the feeling that I was letting my family down. My wife, Shelly's, part-time nursing income helped us provide for Kelsey, three, and Tanner, one, but I was the main bread winner. A month after changing jobs, I now wondered if I had made the right choice.

Shelly had supported my decision to take a pay cut with the promise of a greater opportunity for advancement in the future. Yet the reality of a smaller paycheck was hard to swallow. Many sleepless nights and much prayer had gone into the decision, but now I questioned it.

Pulling into the driveway just before 9 p.m., I was surprised to see Tanner still awake in his carseat. It was past his bedtime and car rides usually put him right to sleep. Shelly got Kelsey ready for bed, while I tried to settle Tanner down. Two hours later, Tanner was still wide awake. I was tired and feeling as cranky as he was behaving. None of the usual tricks would settle him down.

"I need to get some rest," I thought looking at the clock. Desperate, I buckled him back into his car seat hoping a little drive would put him to sleep. Pulling onto the street, I turned on the car CD player. Nothing happened. I pushed all the buttons. Still nothing. The CD changer was a unit that held a cartridge of ten CD's. It was installed in the trunk and operated by the car radio buttons on the dashboard. I had worked in the car stereo business for six years and had installed it myself. "It was just working perfectly on the way home," I thought and switched to the radio.

Within two blocks, Tanner's reflection in the rearview mirror revealed sleep had finally won out. I returned home and put him to bed. Although I knew I needed sleep too, I crept back to the car to take a look at the CD player.

As I opened the trunk, shivers went down my spine. The cartridge had ejected a full eighteen inches onto a big box of frozen meats my in-laws had given us that evening to help us with grocery expenses. All the steaks, chickens, and ground meat would have been spoiled if they had sat forgotten in the hot car trunk all night.

Normally, the only way to eject the cartridge was to push the button on the inside of the trunk. And even then, the CD would only slide out less than two inches— not eighteen. There was no logical explanation as to how the cartridge could have popped out on its own and landed a foot and a half away. This was no freak accident; it was God's grace. We really needed those meats to help us through the coming month. Now I realized I also needed to trust that God would take care of us.

— Darin Rusch

Darin Rusch is the active father of six children, five girls and one boy. When Darin is not working as an outside sales person for an electric distributor near his home in Bismarck, North Dakota, he spends time coaching his son's hockey team. Darin enjoys woodworking and taking walks with his kids.

Good Will Come from Evil

Dachau, 1942. Prisoner 22104 was too weak to lift a shovel, yet he was building a road for the Third Reich. When he collapsed in the mud, he prayed for death.

The guard stood over him. "I could kill you now—you are of no use," he said. "But you will be dead soon anyway." The guard moved on.

The prisoner then heard some noise behind a nearby fence. He could see a German girl, ten or eleven, picking up apples that had fallen from the trees. After the guard moved away, she threw some apples toward the prisoner. He reached through the fence and picked one up.

"We have no bread at home," she said in a low voice, "but I will be going soon to the bakery and will bring you some."

An hour later when the child returned, the prisoner still lay by the fence. When she saw the guard was not watching, she threw a piece of bread. It was still warm.

"This was the moment," says Monsignor Joseph Gluszek, "that I stopped praying for death and started praying for life. I realized that even in Germany there were still human beings who were good."

Gluszek grew up in a village in what is now southern Poland. His family had a few acres of land, two cows, some chickens, and a few pigs. After the first World War, his father came home suffering from malaria. In four years, the man was dead.

After the funeral, young Joseph Gluszek lingered beside his father's grave. An older man visiting the cemetery that day noticed him. Talking to the youth, he learned that with the death of his father, the lad's education would end. "I want to talk to your mother," the older man said.

"This good Christian man, who had no children of his own, wanted to do something for another," says Gluszek. "Thanks to him, I was able to finish college and go to the University of Krakow. He took care of all my expenses until I was ordained a priest."

Gluszek, ordained in Krakow in 1935, was assigned to a village in the mountains of southern Poland. But his peaceful life there ended abruptly on September 1, 1939, when Germany invaded Poland. The very first day of the war, the Nazis arrested the young priest and took him in chains from Poland to Czechoslovakia. Then he was sent to Germany, to the concentration camp at Dachau.

"Jews, Gypsies, and priests," he says. "These were the three categories destined to die in the concentration camp. They got rid of the Jews and the Gypsies first. About 400 Polish priests survived out of the 1,300 there."

Two-and-a-half years after the apple incident, the prisoners at Dachau learned of an order for their extermination. Heinrich Himmler, head of the Gestapo, did not want the advancing American troops to find any prisoners. And so, at 9 p.m. on April 29, 1945, the local S.S. were ordered to machine-gun every prisoner, burn the camp, and move into the Alps.

"But God had different plans for us," says Gluszek. "That very Sunday, at four in the afternoon, good General Patton liberated the camp." Gluszek had spent nearly the entire war inside the camp.

"It wasn't easy being at Dachau," he says. Though thousands survived, millions did not. The victorious Americans and British undertook the welfare of those who remained, including slave laborers conscripted for the German war machine, and put them in displaced persons camps. Gluszek was assigned to one of these camps, and he ended up serving as the lone chaplain for 11,000 Polish young people who had been snatched from the schools and streets of Poland.

The end of the war did not bring peace to Europe. Later, Gluszek watched from his camp as the Soviet Union cut off all rail, water, and highway routes through East Germany to West Berlin. He knew then that he did not want to go back to a Poland that would be under the control of such an oppressive regime.

But to come to America, Gluszek's dream, a priest would need the sponsorship of an American bishop. And the truth is, it wasn't easy to find a bishop to take a concentration camp survivor. "I don't blame them," he says. "After five or six years in the camps, survivors needed therapy to become normal again." One day, though, an American priest from Chicago visited the displaced person's camp. The priest found out that Gluszek had been a priest in the village from which the U.S. priest's own mother had immigrated to America. After the American priest continued on to Rome, he met William J. Condon, bishop of the Diocese of Great Falls, Montana. He told the bishop about Gluszek.

"So in 1950, after nine days in a small Army boat, I arrived in New York," Gluszek explains. "For the first time, I could see the Statue of Liberty. Everyone on the boat had tears in their eyes."

Still, it wasn't easy at first. Gluszek could speak German, Polish, Bohemian, and some Spanish. But he couldn't speak English. People were kind, though, and he learned quickly. He served first in Red Lodge, then in Billings. After only two years, he was assigned his own parish and later ministered at several others.

When he turned seventy, Monsignor Gluszek retired to Holy Family Parish in Great Falls. Since then, he's taken care of the local nursing homes. "I'm just so happy I am serving these precious people," he says. "I don't do anything special. I'm just an ordinary priest."

Though serving as a priest in the Diocese of Great Falls, Gluszek remains listed on the rolls in Krakow, where he was ordained. Indeed, during his early years in Montana, Gluszek kept in communication with Bishop Karol Wojtyla of Krakow. It was Wojtyla, in fact, who asked Pope Paul VI to name Gluszek a monsignor in 1971.

In 1976, Karol Wojtyla, by then a cardinal, came to the Eucharistic Congress in Philadelphia. Before returning to Poland, he wanted to go to Montana to visit the priest with whom he'd corresponded for so many years. Consequently, Wojtyla and Gluszek celebrated Mass together.

"We didn't know then that he was the one God had in mind to be the Pope," Monsignor Gluszek says. But two years later, Gluszek found himself traveling to Rome to attend the installation of Pope John Paul 11.

Since then, Gluszek has been to Rome a half dozen times. "I have been privileged to be invited to be with the Pope, to celebrate Mass with him, to share food with him," Gluszek says.

As he looks back over his life, Gluszek understands how important the small moments in one's life are. A kind stranger in a cemetery, a child whose name he never heard, a famous general, a priest visiting a displaced person's camp, and a caring cardinal destined for the highest office in the Church—all profoundly changed his life.

— Bernice Karnop

Bernice Karnop lives in Montana and writes for the Montana Senior Citizen News.

Lifting Spirits

Taking a long, deep breath, I inhaled the smell of freshly-mowed grass on a beautiful day in May. Working in my yard after work always brings me a sense of peace and relaxation, but this year it also brought a touch of sadness. My only brother, Gary, had died five months earlier at the age of fifty-six. He had always taken pleasure in keeping his yard in tip-top shape. I could not help thinking of him as I raked up the grass clippings. Gary was eighteen years my senior, but we had been close. I really missed him.

"The yard's looking good," a familiar voice called, breaking my reverie. It was my neighbor from across the street, Dorlyn Desens.

"Say, with Zach getting bigger, have you thought of eventually getting a van with a lift?" Dorlyn had watched us lift our eleven-year-old son, Zach, in and out of our van many times.

Zach has spina bifida. His spinal cord never developed fully so he needs to use a wheel chair. At 6' 3" it was not a big problem for me, but my 5' 3" wife, Tammy, was beginning to struggle a little.

"Yes," I answered my neighbor. "We have thought about getting one, but we plan on paying off our other car first."

My income as a police officer and Tammy's as a secretary enabled us to provide well for Zach and our daughter fifteen-year old daughter, Jenna, but we still needed to budget carefully.

"You really need to see this van," Dorlyn persisted. "It was owned by my cousin before he died this past January. I think you can get a really good deal."

"Why not?" I gave in. "It can't hurt to look—you never know ... "

The next day, Tammy and I followed Dorlyn the eleven miles to Rainy Lake where the van, which had belonged to David Perling, was parked. David was born in International Falls, Minnesota, the town in which we now lived. When he was fifteen, he had an accident which left him paralyzed. David went on to become an electrical engineer and moved to Arizona where he lived for thirty years with his wife, Marlene. Six years ago they bought a place on Rainy Lake, just a few miles away from International Falls, where they could escape Arizona's searing summer heat. After his fatal stroke in January, Marlene could not imagine returning to their summer get-away without him.

Tammy and I looked over the van. It was in great shape—no rust, low miles, and the motorized lift would be nice. I looked at Tammy and we both agreed that we had better pay off our car before we start seriously looking into this type of purchase.

"Let me show you the pontoon boat too," Dorlyn said, and I thought "Why not?" Who could pass up an excuse to stay a little longer on beautiful Rainy Lake? It was where my brother, Gary, had requested his ashes to be scattered.

The pontoon boat was something I dared not even dream of owning. Equipped with a ramp and a sturdy, level surface, it would be perfect for Zach, who was unable to go out on a boat because of the difficulty in getting him on one. A pontoon like this would solve the problem, but a purchase was just not realistic given our family finances.

"Come and see the house too," Dorlyn said. An enthusiastic man, his request was hard to turn down. The four-level completely handicapped-accessible home was incredible: completely modernized, wide decks, an elevator, and big picture windows to bring the panoramic vista inside.

Tammy and I "oohed" and "aahed" as we admired a home the likes of which we had never seen before.

Sounding very much like a real estate agent, Dorlyn asked, "Now couldn't you just picture yourself living here?"

No, I couldn't. Some things you do not even imagine. I laughed and said, "In our dreams."

"Maybe if we won the lottery," Tammy said, also laughing.

"Well, let's call Marlene and see what kind of price we can get on the van," Darlyn suggested. He handed Tammy a cordless extension and dialed up the other phone for me.

"So how did you like the van?" Marlene asked.

"We loved it," I admitted.

"I realize you have a son in a wheelchair. My husband had to use one so I know what it's like. I would like to just give you the van."

Tammy and I exchanged unbelieving expressions. "Are you sure?" I asked. Tammy gently asked her repeat her offer; she could not believe what she had just heard.

Marlene assured us we heard correctly. Then she asked us what we thought of the boat. Did Zach like fishing, she wanted to know.

In spite of his disabilities, Zach was a happy-go-lucky kid who liked everything—even school. Yes, he liked fishing, but it was not something he had much opportunity to do.

"I want to give you the boat too," Marlene said.

Tammy and I were stunned. "You must be kidding,"

I whispered, almost inaudibly. By now I had to sit down, I was weak and shaking from the shock of it all.

"No, I have the means and I want to do this," she insisted. "David and I had so much enjoyment on the lake. The property meant so much to him. I could never put a price on any of it. To me, it's just priceless," she continued. "But I could never come up without David. I cried a ton of tears and I know I could never sell the place. I prayed for an answer to my problem and that's when it came to me. I asked God to show me a family who could benefit from this and I want you to have it all; the van, the boat, the house, and everything in it."

Tammy started crying and by then, I was shaking and absolutely speechless. Dorlyn looked at us with a grin that reached ear to ear. We were in shock.

"Thank you" seemed so inadequate a thing to say but I could think of nothing else. The drive home was a blur. We stopped off to see my father-in-law and asked him if this seemed possible. There was a part of us that could not comprehend it all. That evening we called Dorlyn.

"Dorlyn," I asked. "Is this real?"

He said it was.

Zach and Jenna were in shock too.

"On the lake?" Zach asked, incredulously. "Is this really possible?"

Tammy and I kept waiting to wake up from the dream, but instead, we are now waking up on the beautiful Rainy Lake every morning in a home that was specially created for someone like our son. Today, only one month later, it still feels like we are on vacation or living some one else's incredible life.

As impossible as all these extraordinary gifts seemed to Marlene and me, we believe that God has orchestrated everything. When we first learned of Zach's disability, life was never the same again. After the initial devastation, we began to see almost immediately that God had a plan for us and that both our children. Through Zach's disability our family grew in love and spirituality in ways not possible without his disability. And now, these gifts had been given to us through him.

A couple days after we moved into our dream home, my daughter looked at a print hanging on a wall in the den and called out, "Dad, there's uncle Gary!"

I looked at the print made a couple years ago for an all-class reunion. It was a collage of pictures. In a corner of the print was my brother Gary in his hockey uniform celebrating his high school team's 1965 hockey championship. Seeing my brother's face on the wall of our new home, a deep sense of peace shot through me. I felt touched by the hand of God. God had made so many connections for us.

As I sat on the deck of few days later watching two eagles soar overhead, I again experienced that sense of peace. Looking at the two majestic birds, it felt as though Gary and David were looking down on us. And along with our Heavenly Father, they were watching and smiling lovingly upon our family.

— Terry Wood

Terry Wood is a police officer of eighteen years. He lives in International Falls, Minnesota, with his wife of eighteen years, Tammy, and their two children, Jenna (fifteen) and Zach (eleven). Terry's true joy in life is spending time with his family on Rainy Lake.

See pictures related to this story at www.AmazingGraceOnLine.net/Heart

In His Image

During a women's Bible study on the book of Malachi, the group studied chapter three, verse three, which says: "He will sit as a refiner and purifier of silver." This verse puzzled the women and they wondered what this meant about the character and nature of God.

One of the women offered to find out about the process of refining silver and get back to the group at their next Bible study. That week, the woman called up a silversmith and made an appointment to watch him at work. She did not mention the reason for her interest in silver beyond her curiosity about the process of refining it.

As she watched the silversmith, he held a piece of silver over the fire and let it heat up. He explained that in refining silver, one needed to hold the silver in the middle of the fire where the flames were hottest so as to burn away all the impurities. The woman thought about God holding us in such a hot spot, then she thought again about the verse that says, "He sits as a refiner and purifier of silver." She asked the silversmith if it was true that he had to sit there in front of the fire the whole time the silver was being refined.

The man answered that, yes, but he also had to keep his eye on it the entire time it was in the fire. For if the silver was left even a moment too long in the flames, it would be destroyed.

The woman was silent for a moment. Then she asked the silversmith, "How do you know when the silver is refined?" He smiled at her and answered, "Oh, that's the easy part—when I see my image reflected in it."

If today you are feeling the heat of the fire, remember that God has His eye on you and will keep His hand on you and watch over you until He sees His image in you.

— Author unknown

Acknowledgements

Many thanks to:

- All the **contributors** who shared their faith, inspiration, hope, and humor with us and our readers.

- **Christine Trollinger** for her excellent articles. What a life you have lived!

- **Glenn Bernhardt** for his many wonderful and humorous cartoon illustrations.

- **Michael Flickinger**, **Tracy Moran**, **Lucy Scholand**, and **Jennifer Taylor** for their editorial assistance.

- **Mike Jones** and the staff at Ave Maria Radio and *Credo* for the articles by Nick Thomm, Jay Copp, and Diane Morey Hanson. To learn more, visit www.avemariaradio.net and www.credopub.com.

- **Beliefnet.com**, which was the source of several of the jokes used.

- **Kinsey Caruth**, for his cover design, and to **Cheryl Vaca** and **Mike Fontecchio** for their typesetting expertise.

- **Helen Coleman** of *Catholic Digest* and **Mimi Roarke** of *Marian Helper* magazine for their assistance.

— Jeff Cavins, Matthew Pinto, and Patti Maguire Armstrong

Editor and Contributor Contact Information

To contact one of the contributors, please write them at the following address:

(Name of writer)
c/o Ascension Press
P.O. Box 1990
West Chester, PA 19380

Or by e-mail:
AmazingGrace@ascensionpress.com

To contact one of the co-editors, please write them at one of the following addresses:

Jeff Cavins
P.O. Box 1533
Maple Grove, MN 55311
Or at: jcavins@attbi.com

Matthew Pinto
P.O. Box 1990
West Chester, PA 19380
Or at: mpinto@ascensionpress.com

Patti Maguire Armstrong
P.O. Box 1532
Bismarck, ND 58502
Or at: patti@bis.midco.net

About the Editors

Jeff Cavins served as a Protestant minister for twelve years before returning to the Catholic faith. His story is chronicled in his autobiography, *My Life on the Rock* (Ascension Press). Jeff is best-known as the founding host of the popular EWTN television program "Life on the Rock." With Matthew Pinto, he is the co-creator of the *Amazing Grace* series of books. He is also the creator and principal author of *The Great Adventure*, a popular Bible study program. Jeff and his wife, Emily, reside in Minnesota with their three daughters.

Matthew Pinto is the author of the best-selling question-and-answer book *Did Adam & Eve Have Belly Buttons?* (Ascension Press), and is the creator of the *Friendly Defenders Catholic Flash Cards* series. Matt is co-founder of several Catholic organizations, including CatholicExchange.com and *Envoy* magazine, and the creator, with Jeff Cavins, of the *Amazing Grace* series of books. Matt and his wife, Maryanne, live in Pennsylvania with their four children.

Patti Maguire Armstrong is the mother of eight children. She worked in the fields of social work and public administration before staying home full-time to raise her children. As a freelance writer, Patti has written more than 400 published articles for both secular and religious publications. She has authored the book *Catholic Truths for Our Children* (www.raising-catholickids.com) as a guide to help parents pass on the Catholic faith to their children. Patti and her husband, Mark, live in North Dakota, where they home school their children until high school. They are also raising a foster child from Kenya.